THE WADSWORTH ENGLISH FOR ACADEMIC PURPOSES SERIES

Series Editors:
Charles H. Blatchford, Fair Oaks, California
Jerry L. Messec, Florida State University

Academically Speaking
Janet Kayfetz, University of California, Santa Barbara
Randy Stice, Nova University, Florida

Academic Writing Workshop
Sarah Benesch, College of Staten Island, CUNY
Mia Rakijas, New York City, New York
Betsy Rorschach, City College, CUNY

Academic Writing Workshop II
Sarah Benesch, College of Staten Island, CUNY
Betsy Rorschach, City College, CUNY

English on Campus: A Listening Sampler
Gary James, Honolulu Community College
Charles G. Whitley, Chaminade University of Honolulu
Sharon Bode, Bradenton, Florida

Overheard and Understood
Sharon Bode, Bradenton, Florida
Sandra Moulding Lee, Linfield College

Improving the Grammar of Written English: The Handbook
Patricia Byrd, Georgia State University
Beverly Benson, DeKalb College

Improving the Grammar of Written English: The Editing Process
Beverly Benson, DeKalb College
Patricia Byrd, Georgia State University

Understanding Conversations
Catherine Tansey, Tokyo, Japan
Charles H. Blatchford, Fair Oaks, California

English on Campus: A Listening Sampler

Gary James
Honolulu Community College

Charles G. Whitley
Chaminade University of Honolulu

Sharon Bode

Wadsworth Publishing Company
Belmont, California
A Division of Wadsworth, Inc.

Dedication

Paul Ban

Bruce Gareth Chen

Linda McAlister

Series Editors: Charles H. Blatchford and Jerry L. Messec
English/ESL Editor: Angela Gantner
Editorial Assistant: Julie Johnson
Managing Designer: Carolyn Deacy
Print Buyer: Karen Hunt
Designer: Andrew H. Ogus
Illustrator: Pamela Kustermann
Compositor: Eastern Graphics
Cover: Bruce Davidson/Magnum Photos

Printed in the United States of America   49

1 2 3 4 5 6 7 8 9 10——94 93 92 91 90

Library of Congress Cataloging-in-Publication Data

James, Gary, 1939–
   English on campus: a listening sampler / Gary James, Charles G. Whitley, Sharon Bode.
      p.   cm. — (The Wadsworth English for academic purposes series)
   ISBN 0-534-10314-6
   1. English language—Textbooks for foreign speakers.
2. Listening.   I. Whitley, Charles G.   II. Bode, Sharon.
III. Title.   IV. Series.
PE1128.J28   1990
428.3′4—dc20
                                                              89-33113
                                                                   CIP

About the Wadsworth EAP Series

The Wadsworth English for Academic Purposes (EAP) series provides appropriate learning materials for university courses that focus on the academic uses of English. The EAP series has been planned to help ESL students communicate competently in all aspects of academic life in the United States. The materials support learning of academic-level skills in reading, writing, listening, and speaking. They can be used in intensive or nonintensive formats, in classroom, group, or individual study, and for courses of varying lengths.

The Wadsworth EAP series is based on three principles:

1. **Comprehensive Skills Development:** The series views language skills as integrated, so each book not only stands on its own but also builds on and relates to other texts in the series. Books targeted for all skill areas maintain a consistent yet nonrepetitive approach.

2. **Academic Community Context:** The series provides practice in the varied language uses that students will encounter in their academic careers. Teaching and learning activities are in the context of college or university classroom or campus life. This context-specific approach respects the learning skills and educational background of students at academic English centers.

3. **Student-Centered, Process-Oriented Materials:** The series places student learning activities at the heart of each lesson and requires

students to take responsibility for their active role in the learning process.

The components of the Wadsworth EAP series include:

—**A grammar reference guide and handbook** that encourages students to identify specific grammar problems and practice language appropriate to specific academic contexts.

—**Listening comprehension texts and tapes** that develop listening skills to the high level necessary for achievement in an academic program.

—**Reading skill development books** that provide opportunity to practice the skills needed to read authentic academic texts with purpose and understanding.

—**Progressive process-oriented writing texts** that develop academic writing skills from brief reports to rigorous research tasks.

—**Spoken language texts** that provide progressive communicative practice to the level demanded of international students in academic programs.

The authors of the Wadsworth EAP series are experienced teachers in academic programs and have developed their materials from their classroom experience. However, the series is not "teacher-proof." The books do not attempt to provide all the "correct" answers, nor do they set down a strict step-by-step approach. The ambiguity of language at this level and the importance of developing interpretative skills are emphasized by the authors.

Although no one book is ideal for all students (or for all teachers), these books will stimulate and encourage everyone who is willing to participate fully in student-centered classes. The authors have written books that they hope will broaden students' vision and empower them with the expanding possibilities of language.

Control and support must come not only from the books themselves but also from the teachers who work with students and from the students themselves who strive to become responsible for their learning. Just as students seek to make the language serve their needs, so teachers need to use materials to support their individual pedagogical styles and approaches to language-learning problems.

In sum, the Wadsworth EAP series seeks to do more than prepare students for an examination in language skills. It seeks to help international students master academic English in order to achieve their academic goals. The authors of these texts have shared their experiences in providing opportunities for students to fulfill their academic potential— and isn't that what each of us would like to achieve?

Charles H. Blatchford and Jerry L. Messec
Series Editors

Contents

Preface   xv

A Note to Teachers on the Exercises in Each Unit   xxii

Introduction for Students   xxxiii

PART ONE   1

Unit 1/Math Graduates   3

Before You Listen   4

As You Listen   4

After You Listen   6

Unit 2/The Hydrologic Process   7

Before You Listen   8

As You Listen   8

After You Listen   10

Unit 3/Life Expectancy   13

Before You Listen   14
As You Listen   14
After You Listen   16

Unit 4/World Energy Sources   17

Before You Listen   18
As You Listen   18
After You Listen   20

Unit 5/Population Movements   21

Before You Listen   22
As You Listen   22
After You Listen   24

Unit 6/A Child's Motor Skills   27

Before You Listen   28
As You Listen   28
After You Listen   30

Unit 7/Completing High School   33

Before You Listen   34
As You Listen   34
After You Listen   36

Unit 8/Large Families   39

Before You Listen   40
As You Listen   40
After You Listen   42

Unit 9/A Cracker House   45

Before You Listen   46
As You Listen   46
After You Listen   48

Unit 10/Immigration to Hawaii   51

Before You Listen   52
As You Listen   52
After You Listen   54

Unit 11/The Demographic Transition   57

Before You Listen   58
As You Listen   58
After You Listen   60

Unit 12/The Advantages of Exporting   63

Before You Listen   64
As You Listen   64
After You Listen   66

Unit 13/Government Expenditures   69

Before You Listen   70
As You Listen   70
After You Listen   72

Unit 14/Ecosystems   75

Before You Listen   76
As You Listen   76
After You Listen   78

Unit 15/International Student Survey   81

Before You Listen   82
As You Listen   82
After You Listen   84

Unit 16/Jobs for Women and Men   87

Before You Listen   88
As You Listen   88
After You Listen   90

Unit 17/USA Today   93

Before You Listen   94
As You Listen   94
After You Listen   96

Unit 18/Adjusting to College Life   99

Before You Listen   100
As You Listen   100
After You Listen   102

Unit 19/Recycling Waste Water   105

Before You Listen   106
As You Listen   106
After You Listen   109

Unit 20/The Scientific Method   113

Before You Listen   114
As You Listen   114
After You Listen   116

PART TWO   119

Unit 21/Persuasion in Speaking   121

Before You Listen   122
As You Listen   122
After You Listen   124

Unit 22/The Basic Accounting Formula   125

Before You Listen   126
As You Listen   126
After You Listen   128

Unit 23/Nutrition   131

Before You Listen   132
As You Listen   132
After You Listen   134

Unit 24/The Law of Demand   137

Before You Listen   138
As You Listen   138
After You Listen   140

Unit 25/The Judicial System   141

Before You Listen   142
As You Listen   142
After You Listen   144

TAPESCRIPTS   145

Unit 1/Math Graduates   147
Unit 2/The Hydrologic Process   147
Unit 3/Life Expectancy   148
Unit 4/World Energy Sources   149
Unit 5/Population Movements   150
Unit 6/A Child's Motor Skills   151
Unit 7/Completing High School   152
Unit 8/Large Families   153
Unit 9/A Cracker House   154
Unit 10/Immigration to Hawaii   155
Unit 11/The Demographic Transition   156

Unit 12/The Advantages of Exporting   157
Unit 13/Government Expenditures   158
Unit 14/Ecosystems   159
Unit 15/International Student Survey   160
Unit 16/Jobs for Women and Men   162
Unit 17/USA Today   163
Unit 18/Adjusting to College Life   164
Unit 19/Recycling Waste Water   166
Unit 20/The Scientific Method   167
Unit 21/Persuasion in Speaking   169
Unit 22/The Basic Accounting Formula   172
Unit 23/Nutrition   175
Unit 24/The Law of Demand   179
Unit 25/The Judicial System   181

ANSWER KEY   185

Unit 1/Math Graduates   187
Unit 2/The Hydrologic Process   188
Unit 3/Life Expectancy   189
Unit 4/World Energy Sources   190
Unit 5/Population Movements   192
Unit 6/A Child's Motor Skills   193
Unit 7/Completing High School   194
Unit 8/Large Families   196
Unit 9/A Cracker House   197
Unit 10/Immigration to Hawaii   198
Unit 11/The Demographic Transition   200
Unit 12/The Advantages of Exporting   201
Unit 13/Government Expenditures   203
Unit 14/Ecosystems   204
Unit 15/International Student Survey   206
Unit 16/Jobs for Women and Men   207
Unit 17/USA Today   209
Unit 18/Adjusting to College Life   211
Unit 19/Recycling Waste Water   213
Unit 20/The Scientific Method   214

Unit 21/Persuasion in Speaking   216

Unit 22/The Basic Accounting Formula   217

Unit 23/Nutrition   219

Unit 24/The Law of Demand   220

Unit 25/The Judicial System   222

Preface

Purpose

This material was written for, and has been used successfully with, international students who are planning to enroll in, or are already enrolled in, a university-level academic program of study in the United States. It was written to help fill the almost desperate need for academically oriented ESL listening material that sounds natural and, at the same time, is relatively easy to work with in the ESL classroom. It can be used with students who represent a wide range of proficiency levels from low intermediate through advanced. Each unit of this text is built around a recorded listening passage. Both the language used in the recorded listening passages and the content of the recorded passages are of the kind heard in classroom lectures, discussions, counseling sessions, and so on in American colleges and universities.

Specifically the purpose of this material is as follows:

1. To improve general listening skills of ESL students in an academic environment.

2. To help students learn to pull out both the main points and the supporting details from something that they've heard.

3. To introduce students to note-taking in English and to give them practice in making notes.

4. To provide a large number of suggested out-of-the-classroom projects that students can participate in and report on.

5. To provide discussion subjects that allow students opportunities to share, in English, their own opinions and feelings.

Nature and Purpose of the Recordings of Class Presentations

The recordings of class presentations were made by 12 different American English speakers who teach a variety of subjects at the college level. Six are male and six are female.

As much as possible, these recordings were designed to sound like real pieces of ongoing classroom activities at an American university. There are a number of reasons for this. One was to give a feeling of actually being in a classroom. Another was to try to capture on tape the kind of natural, not-exactly-perfect language that might occur in that kind of situation. This means that even though the instructors who were doing the recordings had a general idea of what they would say, the language they used was unscripted and often improvised at that time, and thus the language they produced was natural and often slightly more wordy than language necessary to simply convey the facts. (It is important for ESL students to hear this kind of "padded" language, since learning what to ignore is as critical as any other listening skill.) In short, the authors did not want too-carefully crafted classroom presentations because in real life, often they aren't. The authors did not want too-carefully crafted language because in real life, often it isn't.

The recorded class presentations in Part One of the text are generally short, from one to three minutes long, because short passages are easier to deal with. Important features can be pointed out without overwhelming students with a deluge of language. Short recorded passages can be easily replayed again and again, allowing students to complete small tasks while absorbing the actual language itself. Longer presentations of seven minutes or more can be found in Part Two of the text. These passages are also on videotape and can be secured for copying purposes by writing to Wadsworth.

The main purpose of the recorded class presentations is, of course, to allow students to listen to and deal with very natural English in an academic setting while remaining in a controlled and less stressful environment of an ESL classroom.

Contents of Each Unit

The Recorded Class Presentation: This is a short passage of natural-sounding English of the kind that students might actually hear in a real classroom at an American college or university. (These recordings were mentioned earlier in "Nature of the Recordings.")

Text Materials

Each unit contains suggestions for three overlapping divisions: pre-listening activities, listening activities, and follow-up activities.

Pre-Listening Activities ("Before you listen.")

1. Speaking activity *("What's your opinion?")*

2. Speaking activity *("Can you predict?")*

3. Vocabulary practice *("Do you know these words?")*

Listening Activities ("As you listen.")

3.1 Listening for the vocabulary in the recording of the class presentation.

4. Listening to find out if the predictions were accurate. *("Were you right?")*

5. In written form, identifying paraphrases of the sentence in the recorded class presentation that contains the main focus, or main point, of the recording and then identifying that actual sentence in the recording. ("Identify the focus.")

6. Examining the note form of the focus sentence in the recording and writing, in note form, two paraphrased sentences of the focus. ("Making notes: the focus.")

7. Identifying the supporting details in the recording and writing them in note form. ("Making notes: the supporting details.")

Follow-Up Activities ("After you listen.")

8. Suggestions for student projects. *("Can you find out?")*

9. Suggestions for discussion topics. *("Discussion.")*

Description of Each Part of a Unit

The Recorded Class Presentation: This recording is the core of each unit and every activity in the unit is directly or indirectly related to it.

Text Materials

A variety of activities are included in each unit. These activities will help students improve their listening and note-taking skills, provide ample opportunities for individual and group projects, and encourage students to share their knowledge, their experiences, their opinions, and their feelings in English.

Pre-Listening Activities: Before you listen.

These two discussion questions are to help students begin to think about the topic of the recorded classroom presentation. Neither require any advanced preparation or outside work on the part of the students.

1. *What's your opinion!* This is a very general discussion question and may or may not be directly related to the recorded classroom presentation.

2. *Can you predict!* This question encourages students to draw on whatever knowledge they might already have about the topic of the recorded classroom presentation and is directly tied to that recording.

2.1 The visual. The visual material, reproduced or created to display a particular kind of information, provides context for the recorded classroom presentation. It strengthens students' ability to predict the content of the recording and using this context aids listening to and understanding the content of the recording. Since good visual material distills and organizes complex information, the authors feel that it is particularly useful for highlighting the relationships among pieces of information in a challenging listening passage. In completing charts and so on, a student can demonstrate comprehension of the recorded material.

3. *Do you know these words!* As any ESL instructor knows, mid- and lower-level ESL students can easily be overwhelmed by any continuous stream of spoken English. The authors have found that one way to avoid making students feel overwhelmed when they first hear a continuous stream of speech and to also eventually help make comprehension easier is to focus, at first, on small pieces of the language that will appear in the longer stream of speech. That is the purpose of the vocabulary. (Maureen Weissenrieder makes a similar point in "Listening to the News in Spanish" which appears in *The Modern Language Journal,* 71, i[1987].) The vocabulary items were taken from the recorded class presentation and were generally selected to aid comprehension of the main points of the presentation. This vocabulary practice is organized into two steps. In the first step, which is a dictation and spelling exercise, students listen to the items as they are read; first the item, then the item in context, and then the item again. Students are asked to try to write the item. Finally the item is spelled for them. After all items have been completed, the second step is for students to match each item

with its meaning, which appears in a scrambled list of meanings. After completion of this exercise, the students' first listening task, as they hear the recorded class presentation, is to simply listen for those items.

Listening Activities: As you listen.

During the first listening of the recorded classroom presentation, students are simply following the vocabulary. As listening to the recording continues, students are asked to look at the visual.

4. *Were you right?* After listening to the recording, this question allows students to discuss the accuracy of their predictions.

5. *Identify the focus.* Whether dealing with a listening passage, or even a reading passage, identifying the main point of a passage of material can be quite difficult for many ESL students. For this reason, this information is virtually given to the students. And since the meaning of the passage will not be remembered in the words of the speaker, it is useful to have students observe several ways of expressing the main point.

    This exercise contains four sentences. One of the sentences is taken directly from the recorded class presentation in which it serves as the main focus of the recorded presentation. Two of the other sentences are paraphrases of that focus sentence. The meaning of the remaining sentence has been changed in some way so that it is not a paraphrase of the focus sentence.

    Students are asked to read the four sentences and identify which three have the same meaning and to explain why the remaining sentence is different. Then they are asked to identify the actual sentence that is in the recording. Finally they are asked to try to write one more paraphrase of the focus sentence.

6. *Making notes: the focus.* This exercise calls attention to the focus sentence in the recorded class presentation as it might appear in note form. This sentence is written in note form so that students will have recognition practice with abbreviated forms in this first level.

    Students are asked to tell which words in the sentence are abbreviated, which are left out, and what symbols are used. Finally, they are asked to rewrite the two paraphrased sentences in note form. (Some symbols that are commonly used in taking notes are given on the inside cover of this textbook.)

7. *Making notes: the supporting details.* In this exercise, the details that support the main point of the recorded class presentation are written by students in note form to give practice in the style and content of lecture notes. The recordings cover many topics and frequently the students will be listening for numbers. Taking down the details in note form and completing the chart provide com-

prehension checks and give practice not only in note taking, but also exposure to the language of relationships, regardless of the content of the recorded class presentations.

Follow-Up Activities: After you listen.

8. *Can you find out!* This is a list containing a variety of suggestions for student projects which can be done by individual students or which can be done as group projects and which allow students to pursue topics of their own choosing. Students are generally asked to seek out something and then to report what they found to the class. Listening to these student presentations adds further listening practice to the class.

9. *Discussion.* This activity consists of two discussion suggestions for subjects that students can generally talk about with little or no preparation. Discussions can be done either in small groups or with the whole class together.

   Students need some time in class in which they can just relax and share their thoughts with other students. Not only does this give students an opportunity to relate to others through English, but it also contributes to the cohesiveness of the class itself. And that's an important part of what these discussion suggestions are designed to do.

Acknowledgements

English on Campus: A Listening Sampler has evolved over the past four years. One would think that after collaborating on many previous materials, the creative writing process would become easier, but that has not been the case. Not residing in the same place has caused the greatest difficulty, requiring thousands of miles of travel to be together for work sessions. Innumerable long-distance phone calls were made, adding considerably to the coffers of Ma Bell. Lesson manuscript pages were freely circulated in the mails, causing increased revenue for the Postal Service. Having overcome these considerable obstacles, then, we would like to acknowledge our friends and loved ones whose support and understanding made the difference.

   Of course, without the voices of Paul Ban, George Dixon, Karen Hastings, Lei Lani Hinds, Robert Lansing, Doric Little, Lena Low, Bette Matthews, Linda McAlister, Cathy Miles, Roy Mumme, and Ed Schell, no materials would exist. They were the prime source, so for their efforts we thank them. The expertise and patience of Monte Hickok, Katsumi Ige, and Elton Ogoso, media technicians at Honolulu Community College, made the actual taping of the materials an enjoyable experience for all concerned. Special thanks also go to David Nixon in Fort Myers, Florida for the final audio production of the text.

Initially, Clara Iwata, clerk steno at Honolulu Community College, took on the awesome task of typing first-draft lessons and even copying graphs which accompanied them. She did her usual magnificent job. Eventually, over the years she was joined by June Cabbab, Esther Ikawa, Kathy Langaman, and Arlene Yano.

We are most grateful also to Jean Dale for her work and suggestions on early drafts of the material; to Pamela Kustermann for her art work; to Charley Blatchford, Jerry Messec, and Gloria Hooper, chair of the Language Arts Department at Honolulu Community College; and to Steve Rutter, Angie Gantner, and everyone else at Wadsworth who has labored so diligently to bring this academic series together.

Gary James
Charles G. Whitley
Honolulu, Hawaii

Sharon Bode
Bradenton, Florida

A Note to Teachers on the Exercises in Each Unit

I. Pre-Listening Activities

1. *What's your opinion?*

2. *Can you predict?*
   These two discussions may be done on the same day the recorded class presentation is to be used or on the day before. They may be done in small groups or with the whole class. The teacher may even opt to use the first one as a subject for a short written composition.

3. *Do you know these words?*
   Step 1—Dictation
   Note—Some instructors might opt for not presenting vocabulary in this fashion. One alternative is that vocabulary and glosses could be given out before listening to the class presentation. Another alternative is for vocabulary to be simply ignored initially and taught in context as the instructor might feel is important.

   Dictation Preparation
   a. *Choice one:* The teacher can tell students to take out a sheet of notebook paper and number from one to whatever number of items there are. Students will do the dictation practice on the notebook paper.

Choice two: The teacher can tell students to open the textbook to exercise three. Students will do the dictation directly in the textbook.

b. The teacher reminds the class of the subject of the lesson, which was first brought up when predictions were asked for. The teacher tells the class that the vocabulary items are taken directly from the recorded presentation which they will soon hear. The teacher stresses that this is not a test, it is only a practice exercise.

c. To make the dictation a little easier, the teacher might read through the glosses in the book while students silently read them. To make the dictation a little harder the teacher will not, at this point, read them to the class. In this case, and if dictation is to be done directly in the textbooks, the teacher might ask the students to cover the glosses with a card during dictation practice.

d. The teacher tells the class that they will first hear the vocabulary item in isolation. Then they will hear it in the sentence from the recording. Then they will hear it alone again. They are to try to write only the vocabulary item. After a very short pause, the item will be spelled so that they can make corrections if they need to.

Actual Dictation

e. The teacher reads the dictation using the tape transcript. If this is done, the teacher should read in a natural tone at a natural speed. The item or the sentence can be repeated as many times as the teacher thinks is suitable. And, depending on the class, the teacher may want to add other items to the exercise.

Optional Final Dictation Correction

f. *Choice one:* The students make a final check of their work by having the teacher spell aloud all of the items.
Choice two: The students make a final check of their work by looking at the items that are written on the board. The items are written there either during or after the dictation practice by students or by the teacher.

g. *Choice one:* Students make spelling corrections on their notebook paper and then copy all the items into their textbooks. In this case, the teacher may take the notebook paper and later look over the students' work.
Choice two: Students make spelling corrections on their work that was written directly in their textbooks.

Step 2—Matching items with meanings

a. Students are told to look in their textbooks at the scrambled list of glosses (or meanings) for the vocabulary items.

b. The teacher reads aloud through all the glosses while the class follows.

c. *Choice one:* Students, at their own speed, simply match the items with their meanings.
Choice two: The teacher, by using the transcript, reads through each item and its sentence, providing context for the meaning of each item. Students, while listening, match the items with the meanings.
Choice three: Students request the teacher to read certain sentences to aid them in choosing a meaning.
  Students can work alone, they can work in pairs, or they can work in small groups when matching the vocabulary items with their meanings.
d. The meanings are checked and corrected either by having the teacher read the answers from the answer key or by having students read their answers.

Dictation Follow-Up

a. Since dictation is done, at this point, as a practice exercise and not as a quiz, grades generally aren't given on this work. The teacher might simply indicate looking at the work by making a check mark on the paper or by writing good, fair, etc. Of course, students have a little more incentive to do better work if they know the teacher will actually look at it later.
b. Dictation of the same material can, at a later time, be used as a vocabulary review exercise or as a vocabulary quiz. For example, as a quiz, the teacher can dictate the items and tell students that they must, from memory, correctly spell the item and write what it means.

II. Listening Activities

a. The vocabulary items are now written on the board in the order they appear in the recorded class presentation, which is the order in which they were dictated. The teacher reminds the class of the subject of the recording and tells them in what situation this recording might have been made. For example, the recording used in Unit 1 might have been made in a math class.
b. The teacher tells the class not to worry about understanding everything on the tape just yet. Students are to only listen for the vocabulary items that are written on the board and to follow them as they listen.
c. The teacher plays the recorded class presentation and points to the vocabulary item on the board at the same time it is used on the tape. If necessary, the teacher can be following the transcript. Students are simply listening and looking at the board.

d. The students can listen a second or third time, while following the vocabulary list on the board until the teacher feels that they can, at least, hear each item as it comes up in the recording.

   After one or two plays of the tape, it might be appropriate, with some classes, to stop the machine and review the meaning of the vocabulary items. With other classes this step might not be needed.

4. *Were you right?*

   a. Have students open their textbooks to the visual that accompanies the recorded class presentation. Discuss with them general features of the visual—for example, what it's called, how it looks, what information it might show and how it does this, how many categories it shows, and so on.
   b. The teacher reminds the students of their earlier predictions and possibly writes them on the board.
   c. The teacher tells the class that the tape will be played again. This time students are to listen to try to find out whether their earlier guesses were accurate or not.
   d. The teacher plays the recorded class presentation one to three times while students listen for that information.
   e. The machine is stopped and students discuss the accuracy of their earlier predictions.

5. *Identify the focus.*

   a. The teacher has the students look in their textbooks at exercise five, called *Identify the focus.*
   b. The teacher tells students that three of the four sentences here have similar meanings and that one sentence is different.
   c. The teacher reads the four sentences aloud while students listen and follow in their textbooks.
   d. Students are to now look over and possibly discuss the four sentences and then put a check mark in front of the three sentences that have similar meanings. This can be done either by individuals, by pairs, or in small groups.
   e. The marked sentences are checked and discussed either by students or by the teacher, who can refer to the answer key in the back of the book. Students should clearly understand that even though the sentences might look different, the basic meaning of the three sentences is the same, which is why they are called paraphrases.
   f. Whatever it is that is different about the remaining sentence is discussed until students clearly see that it is not a paraphrase.
   g. One of the three paraphrased sentences was taken directly from the transcript of the recorded class presentation. Students are told to indicate the focus sentence that is made up of exactly the same words as in the recording. The tape is then played a few

times while students decide. If they were working in small groups just before this, they will remain in their groups and make a group decision.

h. Their choice for focus sentence in the recording is discussed.

i. Finally students are asked to try to write another sentence, another paraphrase, with the same meaning as the focus sentence in the recording. A few of these sentences can be written on the board and discussed.

6. *Making notes: the focus.*

a. The teacher has the students look in their textbooks at the focus sentence, written in note form.

b. The students are told that this is the focus, or the main point of what was said in the recorded class presentation.

c. The teacher explains that all the important information in the focus sentence is written in note form. Students are told that this is one way a listener might have written that information down during an actual class presentation.

d. The teacher explains that different people might use different ways of shortening that information for the purpose of quickly writing it down. The way it is shown in the textbook is only one way.

e. The teacher mentions briefly that some of the things that happen when people take notes is that: (1) people abbreviate words, that is, they shorten the words by leaving out some of the letters; (2) people use symbols to represent words or phrases or ideas; and (3) they leave out some unimportant words.

f. The students discuss the form of the focus as it appears in the textbook.

g. The teacher has the students try to reconstruct the abbreviated note form of the focus into a complete sentence.

h. Students are asked to rewrite the two paraphrased sentences in note form. The teacher refers the students to the list of symbols that are commonly used in taking notes, which appears on the inside cover of this textbook.

i. Some of these abbreviated sentences are written on the board and discussed. Again students try to reconstruct them into complete sentences.

7. *Making notes: the supporting details.*

a. Depending on the level of the class, the length of the class period, the amount of discussion, and how the teacher feels about it, this activity can either be done as homework (in a language lab or at home with a tape) or as the next day's in-class activity.

b. The teacher tells the students to look at the exercise in their texts, called *Making notes: the supporting details,* which is exercise seven. The students are told that this represents other important information in the recorded class presentation.

c. The teacher reads the instructions aloud and makes sure students understand what they are to listen for and to write down.

d. Tell them that the information is to be written in note form.

e. The teacher might do a small part of the exercise to demonstrate how it is done and what it should look like.

f. If this activity is done in class, the teacher will play the tape as many times as necessary for the students to get the information down. (They might first use notebook paper and then transfer the work to their textbooks.)

g. If this activity is done outside of class, the teacher will assign it to be done individually as homework. (Or in pairs, groups, or whatever.)

h. If this activity seems, at first, too difficult for the class, the teacher can simply play the tape of the recorded class presentation while the students follow the notes in the answer key. After a couple of times of listening and following the key, the students can then be told to go back and do it themselves without looking at the key.

i. This work is then discussed and checked with the teacher. Students can compare their notes to the notes in the answer key.

j. Students can be asked to reconstruct sentences based on the note forms.

k. As a final step, students are told to fill in the information on the visual in their textbooks. Now and then the teacher will point out that human error will sometimes appear in lecture information. For example, in one of the recorded class presentations, the percentages add up to 101%.

Follow-Up Activities for Exercises 5, 6, and 7

a. The teacher can use the same exercises at a later time for quizzes. At that time all work would be done by individuals.

b. Another way the teacher can test the students' comprehension, at a later date, is to write five or six factual comprehension questions based on the focus and the supporting details as given in the recorded class presentation.

c. To test this way, the teacher tells students to take out two sheets of paper and a pencil. One sheet of paper is used for note-taking while the recorded class presentation is played. The other sheet is to be used as an answer sheet.

d. After students have listened to the tape and made notes, the teacher reads the earlier-written factual comprehension questions one at a time and students write (long or short) answers on the answer sheet while referring to the notes they just made.

III. Follow-Up Activities

8. *Can you find out?*

   a. The teacher has students, either as individuals or in small groups, read through the list of suggested activities and choose any one that seems interesting.
   b. The teacher tells students that the projects must be finished within a specific amount of time, usually a few days, and assigns a day in the future in which a report on each project will be presented to the class.
   c. If appropriate, the teacher can ask each individual, or each group, to use the following presentation guide, or one with modifications, to help the students clearly let the teacher know what is to be done.
   d. When reports are given to the class, the teacher can have students take notes on what is being reported and immediately follow up with comprehension questions directed at the class based on notes taken by the teacher. Or the teacher can have students write (or give orally) a brief summary of the report.
   e. The teacher can encourage a question and answer period after each project report. The questions from students are directed at the person or persons who presented the report and are to clarify inmation and to ask for more.
   f. The class can have an open discussion based on the subject of the report.
   g. As far as a possible additional project, both teacher and students should be aware of the wealth of material that is now available on home video. Short documentaries or full-length feature films and everything in between can do much to add to the regular classroom format. In addition to video material now available in school libraries, the teacher and the students can visit video rental shops to find out what things are available that might relate to what's being done in the class.

9. *Discussion*

   a. Every few days, the teacher can set aside 10 to 20 minutes of discussion time. Advance preparation on the students' part isn't necessary, but if the teacher thinks preparation is worthwhile, the students are asked to prepare. This might be a short composition based on whatever discussion subject was chosen.
   b. If group members do write a short composition on a topic chosen by their group, a pre-discussion activity can be the sharing of the compositions by the group members. They could either be read aloud to the group or passed around to be read silently. After the three or four compositions are shared, the compositions are given to the teacher and discussion inside the group begins.

Presentation Guide

1. My exact topic is _____

2. I can find the information

   a. from my own experience because _____

   _____

   b. by interviewing _____ because _____

   _____

   c. in the library, and my exact question is _____

3. I will use a graph, chart, map or other visual material to explain _____

   _____

4. I will practice my presentation with _____

Other Notes

_____

_____

_____

_____

_____

c. *Choice one:* One way to handle small-group discussion with no advance preparation is as follows: Students in groups of three or four people are told to read the two suggestions, choose one that seems interesting to all members of the group, and share their feelings about it in relaxed conversation. The teacher has, beforehand, encouraged everyone to participate; here there's no one in charge or no group leader to make sure everyone does. *Choice two:* Another way to handle small-group discussion with no advance preparation is as follows: Students in groups of three or four are told to silently read the two discussion suggestions. Students are told to each silently mark the suggestion he or she likes best.

   Students in each group assign one of the letters A, B, C (and possibly D) to each member of the group. The teacher writes A, B, C on the board and simply circles one of the letters without knowing who, in each group, it represents.

The teacher tells the groups that that person *B*, for example, will be the discussion leader in each group. The teacher explains that the discussion leader is responsible for asking questions, getting participation from all group members, and keeping the conversation going.

The teacher tells each discussion leader to tell his or her group which topic he has chosen for discussion. Group members close their textbooks and the leader starts the discussion. The teacher may or may not ask group leaders to close their books.

d. Discussion itself can be the end purpose of this activity, or, if the teacher thinks it suitable, the class can write a short composition after the discussion in which they summarize what was said in their groups.

IV. General Comments

Suggested Teaching Procedures

The step-by-step suggestions that were just given represent only one of a number of ways these materials can be used. When using a new textbook, it seems useful, at least for a while, to have most things clearly spelled out for the teacher. Some teachers feel good about this as it seems to help give some degree of confidence in using new materials. Others find detailed suggestions of this nature quite restrictive. It seems reasonable to suggest that teachers who use these materials for the first time might, at first, want to follow these suggestions and then, as they become more familiar with the materials, begin to make whatever changes they think are suitable.

It's quite true that, by making certain adjustments, these materials can be used with a wide range of ESL classes from rather low to rather high. For example, in exercise seven, *Making notes: the supporting details*, the suggestion was made to let students see the notes in the answer key while listening to the tape before asking them to write similar ones, if doing that seemed appropriate. In the same way, students in a rather low-level class could be shown the written transcript when they first listen to the recorded class presentation. This, of course, would not be necessary and probably not appropriate in a higher level class.

The only really strong suggestion from the authors to teachers using this material is this: Be creative, and when you come up with different ways of using these materials, share those ideas with us. This can be done by writing to us in care of the publisher. In the future, we may be able to pass these suggestions on to others.

Using the Recorded Classroom Presentation

How does one know the appropriate number of times to play the tape? The answer is this. Repeat the tape as much as necessary to do the specific task called for in each of the listening exercises. One listening may be enough. It may take four or five. Or seven. Underplaying the tape will cause unrest, confusion, and resentment. Overplaying the tape will cause unrest, boredom, and resentment. During this time, the teacher must be sensitive to student reactions. The teacher can always ask simple yes-no questions or discuss certain features of the recording to help gauge whether the students are, at that moment, able to complete the assigned task.

The Teacher's Role and Responsibilities in Using These Materials

Choice one: The teacher can assume the role of autocrat and be totally responsible for everything that transpires in the classroom.

Choice two: The teacher can assume the role of facilitator, thereby sharing responsibility with students for everything that transpires in the classroom. In this case, the teacher plans and conducts classroom activities in such a way that the attention of the class is on students as much or more than on the teacher.

Choice three: The teacher can combine the above two roles by being somewhat autocratic but at the same time giving some responsibility to students.

Whatever role the teacher finds most suitable, there are some general considerations the authors have found to be particularly relevant in using these materials. They are put forth here simply as points to think about and which might be helpful in planning and carrying out class activities as suggested by these materials.

In using these materials, the authors have found it helpful to:
a. Try to gear class activities to the actual level of the class. This means that the starting point is actually where the class is today as opposed to where someone thinks it ought to be. With these materials the successful ESL teacher might be thought of as walking a fine line while doing a balancing act. The teacher tries to avoid teaching too far over the heads of the students while avoiding making the material too easy for the students. Ideally these materials are presented in such a way that seems somewhat difficult for the students but, with some work, is within their reach.
b. Try to keep the pace of the class up; move briskly along from activity to activity. Be flexible and sensitive to what's happening in the classroom. Be alert and change the activity if something isn't working or if the class is getting bored. Be aware that everything the

teacher needs to know about the general mood of the class, how students are reacting, and how much they are getting from a given activity is being sent out by every member of the class all the time. Every good ESL teacher knows that this is the language the teacher learns while helping the students learn English.

c. Try to make it a point to interact with students on an adult level. Speak to them as adults and seriously listen to their opinions. The teacher can (and possibly sometimes should) offer his or her own opinions while stressing that they are opinions only. The teacher emphasizes that everyone in the classroom has an equal right to express opinions and everyone has the responsibility of listening to others' opinions. The teacher points out that we need not get upset when someone disagrees with our opinions in this kind of situation. We can be flattered that that person feels comfortable enough to be honest with us.

d. Try to stress the importance of improvement for the sake of improvement and not for the sake of grades only. Grades might seem very important right now, but sometime in the future the most important thing will be how well students can function in English. In fact it will be absolutely critical. If students can be made aware of that now, their lives will be far easier in the future.

e. Finally, try to have fun in the classroom. Try to create an atmosphere in which everyone can have fun. One thing that most good teachers would probably agree on is that a little enjoyment goes a long way toward helping people learn.

Introduction for Students

One of the reasons you are studying is to get information about something. One important way to get that information is to listen to someone talk about it. This text will help you better understand the language that is used by your instructors in the classroom.

There are twenty-five different lecture excerpts, or pieces, in this text. Take a look at the contents page. Many topics have been included from different subject areas that might interest you. Science, sociology, psychology, economics, and speech are only a few of the subjects covered. We hope that you will follow the title of this book and "sample the academic English." Getting a taste of the kind of English now that you will hear in other classes will help ensure your future academic success. Good luck!

Gary James

Charles G. Whitley

Sharon Bode

PART ONE

Math Graduates

Diploma

Before You Listen

1. What's Your Opinion?

A liberal arts education is designed to give students some degree of knowledge in a broad range of subject areas. Why do you think so many American colleges and universities have programs like that? In your case, what do you think the advantages would be in studying in a liberal arts program? How about disadvantages? Have you ever taken a new class that you expected to dislike but which you actually enjoyed? If so, what was that? What made you change your mind about that class?

2. Can You Predict?

What kinds of jobs do you think students with mathematics degrees actually find? What percentage of math majors do you think get jobs in unrelated fields? Can you guess what the largest single category is?

As You Listen

3. Do You Know These Words?

Listen to some words and phrases taken from part of the class lecture. You will hear each word or phrase in a sentence. You will also hear the spelling. Write down the word or phrase on the lines below. After you finish, find the meanings in the right-hand column.

1. _____

2. _____

3. _____

4. _____

5. _____

a. chief subjects one studies in college

b. having a strong wish to do something

c. having to do with numbers

d. jobs done with the hands

e. office work

Now listen for these words and phrases in the recording. 〔●-●〕

4. Were You Right?

Look at the graph again as you listen to the tape. Was your prediction about the largest category correct? 〔●-●〕

5. *Identify the Focus*

Three sentences below have similar meanings. Put a check mark (✔) next to them. What's different about the remaining sentence? Now listen for the words that focus attention on the main idea in this part of the class presentation. ▣

1. Just because math is your major you're not going to end up in math-related jobs.

2. Since math is your major you will end up with math-related jobs.

3. You're not going to be doing jobs related to mathematics simply because you have a degree in math.

4. Your major is mathematics but you will not necessarily get a job related to your major.

Which words did you actually hear? Can you think of another sentence with the same meaning?

6. *Making Notes: The Focus*

The focus of this part of the class lecture can be written in note form this way:

math maj ≠ math rel jobs

Which words are abbreviated? Which words were left out? What symbols are used?

Now using your own abbreviations and symbols, rewrite sentences three and four. Compare your notes with your classmates.

_____

_____

7. *Making Notes: The Supporting Details*

On the lines below note down the types of jobs math majors find. Also, take down the percentages in each area. ▣

Math-related   *Not Math-related*

_____ ___%   _____ ___%

_____ ___%   _____ ___%

_____ ___%   _____ ___%

_____ ___%   _____ ___%

_____ ___%   _____ ___%

_____ ___%   _____ ___%

After You Listen

8. Can You Find Out?

1. How many students graduate with degrees in your major field? What kinds of jobs do they find?

2. Explain a different number system to your classmates. For example, you might explain the number system of computers.

3. Interview a mathematics teacher. Find out if English is very important for math majors. Report the results of your interview to your classmates.

4. If there is a museum of science and industry in your city, visit the mathematics section.

9. Discussion

1. In general, do you like to study mathematics? What do you like or not like about math? Is math a popular major at universities in your home country? Do you think everyone should be educated in mathematics? Why or why not?

2. Have you already chosen your major field of study? If so, what is it? Did your parents or other family members tell you what to study? Did you choose your major because you like the subject? Did you choose your major because you can easily get a job? Which do you think is more important, a university education that gives students job skills or one that helps to develop the ability to think well? Why?

UNIT 2

The Hydrologic Process

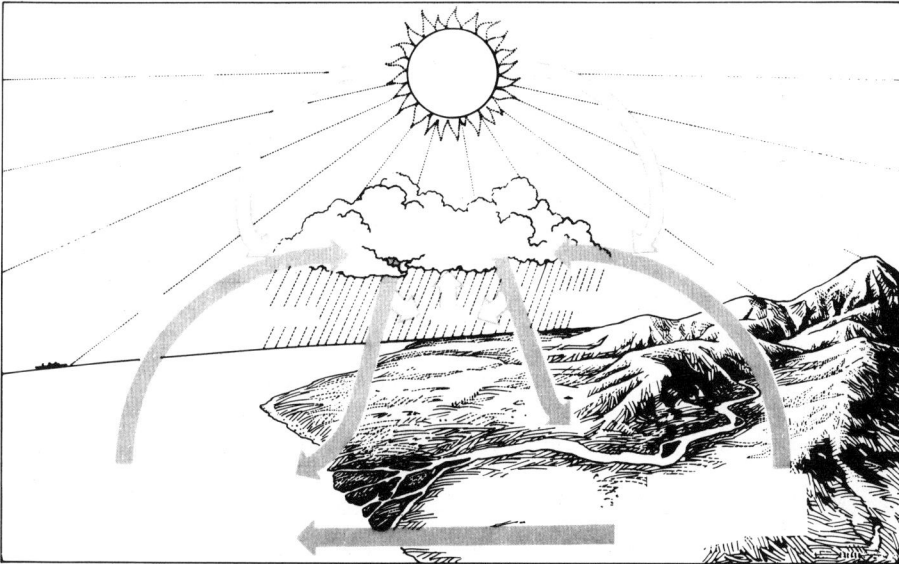

From *Living in the Environment*, Third Edition, by G. Tyler Miller, Jr. © 1982 by Wadsworth, Inc. Reprinted by permission.

Before You Listen

1. What's Your Opinion?

How important is water to your city or country? Do you live in a rainy or a dry area? Where does the water for your house come from? What countries have too much water? too little water?

2. Can You Predict?

Look at the picture of the hydrological (water) cycle. Name the different parts of the picture. Can you explain to your partner how water comes from clouds to the earth and back to clouds again?

As You Listen

3. Do You Know These Words?

Listen to some words and phrases taken from part of the class lecture. You will hear each word or phrase in a sentence. You will also hear the spelling. Write down the word or phrase on the lines below. After you finish, find the meanings in the right-hand column.

1. _____   a. rocks under the earth that hold water

2. _____   b. steam in the air

3. _____   c. the air

4. _____   d. the change of clouds to rain, snow, etc.

5. _____   e. the change of water to steam

6. _____   f. the change of water to steam through plants

7. _____   g. the water cycle from clouds back to clouds again

Now listen for these words and phrases in the recording. 🔲

4. Were You Right?

Look at the picture again as you listen to the recording. Were your predictions about the water cycle accurate? [●-●]

5. Identify the Focus

Three sentences below have similar meanings. Put a check mark (✔) next to them. What is different about the remaining sentence? Now listen for the words that focus attention on the main idea in this part of the class presentation. [●-●]

1. Evaporation and precipitation are the two parts of the hydrological process.

2. The hydrological process is a process of evaporation and precipitation.

3. The water cycle is about the change of water vapor to rain, snow, etc., and back to water again.

4. Water has three forms: ice, water, and steam.

Which words did you actually hear? Can you think of another sentence with the same meaning?

6. Making Notes: The Focus

The focus of this part of the class lecture can be written in note form this way:

hydrologl proc = proc evap ↑ & precip ↓

Which words are abbreviated? Which words were left out? What symbols are used?

Now using your own abbreviations and symbols, rewrite sentences one and three. Compare your notes with your classmates.

_____

_____

7. Making Notes: The Supporting Details

Look at the slides below. On the line below each slide, write down what the slide shows. Use abbreviations and symbols. Then listen to the tape. Number the slides (1, 2, 3 . . .) as you hear each described. Check your answers with your teacher. ▆▬▆

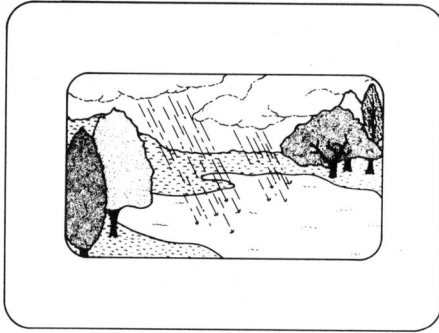

After You Listen

8. Can You Find Out?

1. Interview the weather reporter at a local TV station by phone. Ask about the rain patterns in the local area. Report back to your classmates.

2. Some areas of the world have problems with floods or droughts. Use a map or other visual material to talk about the water situation in your own country.

3. Visit the local water plant. Where does the water come from? How does it get to the houses and businesses in the area? Is the local water supply related to the amount of rain?

4. Invite a geography teacher or natural science teacher to talk to your class. Find out more about the physical history of the local area. How is the weather related to the geography?

5. Listen to a recording of *The Grand Canyon Suite*. Listen to the section called "A Sudden Rainstorm." As you listen, imagine the wind blowing the clouds, the rain falling, the sun coming out again. Can you feel the water vapor as the sun heats the wet ground?

9. *Discussion*

1. Acid rain occurs when industrial pollutants from one area are carried into the atmosphere, mix with water vapor, and then fall with the rain in other areas. Acid rain is considered by many scientists to be a serious threat to forests and to the natural environment. In your opinion, who should be responsible for controlling this? Should it be private industry? Local governments? National governments? What do you think might eventually happen if acid rain is not controlled?

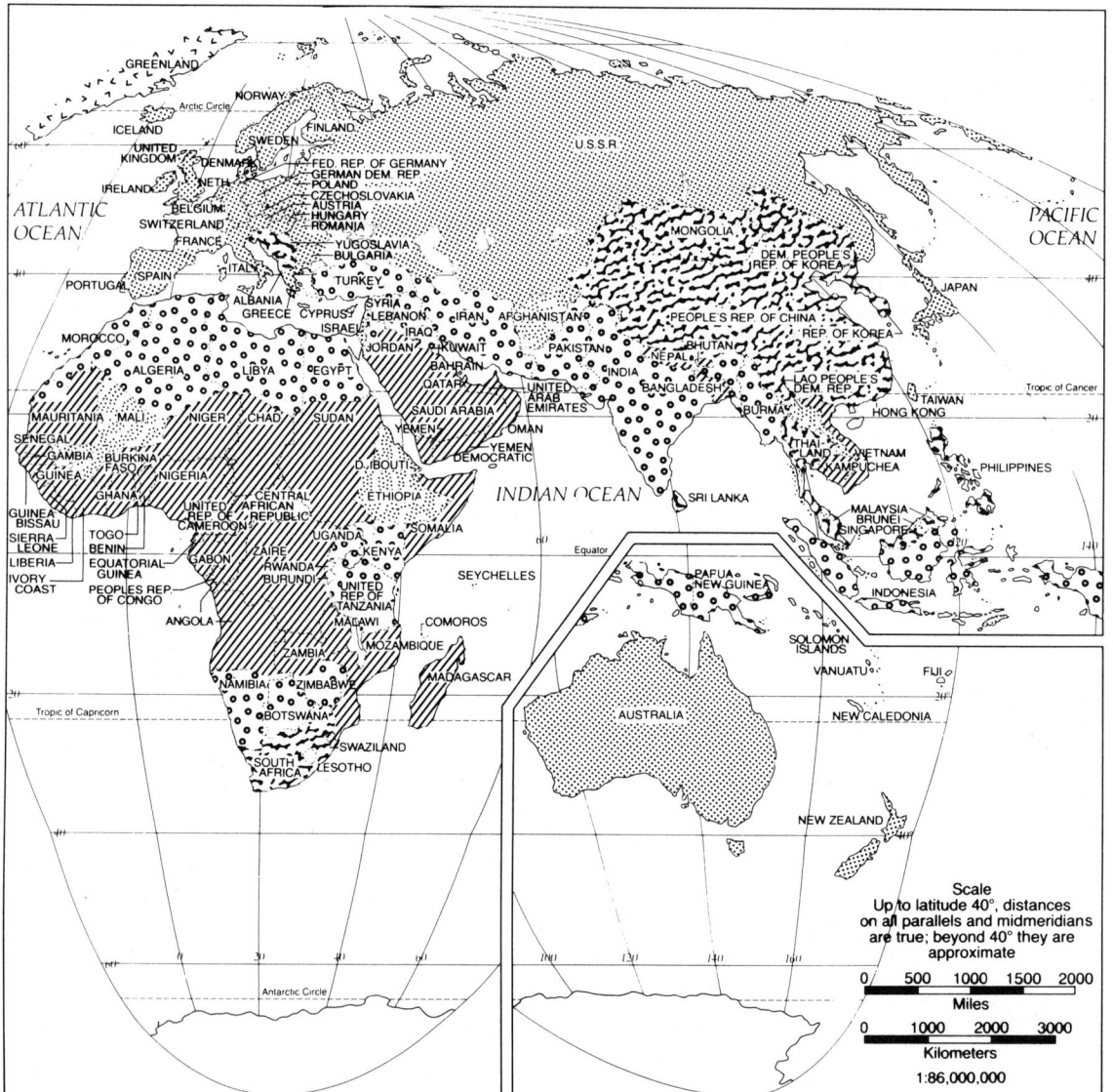

GREENLAND

NORWAY

Arctic Circle

ICELAND

SWEDEN FINLAND

UNITED KINGDOM

DENMARK FED. REP OF GERMANY
GERMAN DEM. REP.
POLAND
CZECHOSLOVAKIA
AUSTRIA
HUNGARY
ROMANIA

U.S.S.R.

IRELAND

NETH.

ATLANTIC OCEAN

PACIFIC OCEAN

BELGIUM
SWITZERLAND
FRANCE

YUGOSLAVIA
BULGARIA

MONGOLIA

DEM. PEOPLE'S REP OF KOREA

ITALY

TURKEY

PORTUGAL SPAIN

ALBANIA
GREECE CYPRUS
SYRIA
LEBANON
ISRAEL
JORDAN

IRAN AFGHANISTAN

PEOPLE'S REP. OF CHINA

JAPAN

REP. OF KOREA

MOROCCO

IRAQ
KUWAIT
BAHRAIN
QATAR

PAKISTAN

NEPAL
BHUTAN

ALGERIA LIBYA EGYPT

SAUDI ARABIA

UNITED
ARAB
EMIRATES

INDIA

BANGLADESH

BURMA

Tropic of Cancer

TAIWAN

HONG KONG

MAURITANIA MALI NIGER CHAD SUDAN

YEMEN

OMAN

LAO PEOPLE'S
DEM. REP.

SENEGAL

YEMEN
DEMOCRATIC

THAI-
LAND

VIETNAM

GAMBIA
GUINEA

BURKINA
FASO

NIGERIA

D. JIBOUTI

INDIAN OCEAN

KAMPUCHEA

PHILIPPINES

GUINEA
BISSAU

GHANA

CENTRAL
AFRICAN
REPUBLIC

ETHIOPIA

SRI LANKA

MALAYSIA

SIERRA
LEONE

TOGO

UNITED
REP. OF
CAMEROON

BRUNEI
SINGAPORE

BENIN

SOMALIA

LIBERIA

EQUATORIAL
GUINEA

GABON

ZAIRE

UGANDA

KENYA

IVORY
COAST

PEOPLES REP.
OF CONGO

RWANDA
BURUNDI

PAPUA
NEW GUINEA

INDONESIA

ANGOLA

UNITED
REP. OF
TANZANIA

SEYCHELLES

Equator

SOLOMON
ISLANDS

MALAWI

COMOROS

ZAMBIA

MOZAMBIQUE

VANUATU

FIJI

NAMIBIA ZIMBABWE

MADAGASCAR

Tropic of Capricorn

BOTSWANA

NEW CALEDONIA

AUSTRALIA

SWAZILAND

SOUTH
AFRICA

LESOTHO

NEW ZEALAND

Antarctic Circle

Scale

Up to latitude 40°, distances
on all parallels and midmeridians
are true; beyond 40° they are
approximate

0   500   1000   1500   2000

Miles

0   1000   2000   3000

Kilometers

1:86,000,000

UNIT 3

Life Expectancy

Reprinted by permission of the University of Chicago.

Before You Listen

1. What's Your Opinion?

Why do people live longer today than 100 years ago? Why do people in some countries live longer than in other countries? In your own country, do people generally live to 40? 50? 60? Why? Make a list of reasons.

2. Can You Predict?

Look at the map of the world. With a partner, identify the continents, regions, and your own countries. Can you predict where people live, on average, "70 or more years"? Do you know where, on average, people only live about "39 years or less"?

As You Listen

3. Do You Know These Words?

Listen to some words and phrases taken from part of the class lecture. You will hear each word or phrase in a sentence. You will also hear the spelling. Write down the word or phrase on the lines below. After you finish, find the meanings in the right-hand column.

1. _____

a. a list of things arranged one under the other

2. _____

b. all the age groups together, from the lowest to the highest

3. _____

c. countries that have food, industry, money

4. _____

d. countries where the people are very poor

5. _____

e. groups

6. _____

f. the average number of years a person will live

Now listen for these words and phrases in the recording. �

4. Were You Right?

Look at the map as you listen to the lecture again. Were your predictions about life expectancy accurate? ▰

5. Identify the Focus

Three sentences below have similar meanings. Put a check mark (✔) next to them. What is different about the remaining sentence? Now listen for the words that focus attention on the main idea in this part of the class presentation. 【●‑●】

1. Life expectancy is all the same around the world.

2. Life expectancy is not the same all around the world.

3. People everywhere on the globe are not expected to live the same number of years.

4. People die at different ages in different countries.

Which words did you actually hear? Can you think of another sentence with the same meaning?

6. Making Notes: The Focus

The focus of this part of the class lecture can be written in note form this way:

life expectancy ≠ wrld

Which words are abbreviated? Which words were left out? What symbols are used?

Now using your own abbreviations and symbols, rewrite sentences three and four. Compare your notes with your classmates.

_____

_____

7. Making Notes: The Supporting Details

Look at the map key below in the left column. As you listen to the tape, finish the key. In the right-hand column, write down the countries or areas the speaker gives as examples. Use abbreviations for your notes. 【●‑●】

After You Listen

8. Can You Find Out?

1. Find out all you can about a group called Live Aid. What is the group's purpose? How did they raise the money? Why did they start? What do you think about projects like Live Aid? Are there other similar groups that you know of?

2. Invite a speaker from the Public Health Department to your class. What programs are there to increase life expectancy? What are the major problems that shorten life expectancy?

3. Find or draw a map of your own country. Tell the class about the different regions. Are some parts richer than other areas? Why?

9. Discussion

1. What responsibilities does a government have to help its poor people? Does one country have a responsibility to help poor people in another country? Why? When?

2. Modern medicine now can give someone a new heart or other body part. Sometimes the new part is made of plastic. How do you feel about living longer in this way? Would you choose to do so? Why?

World Energy Sources

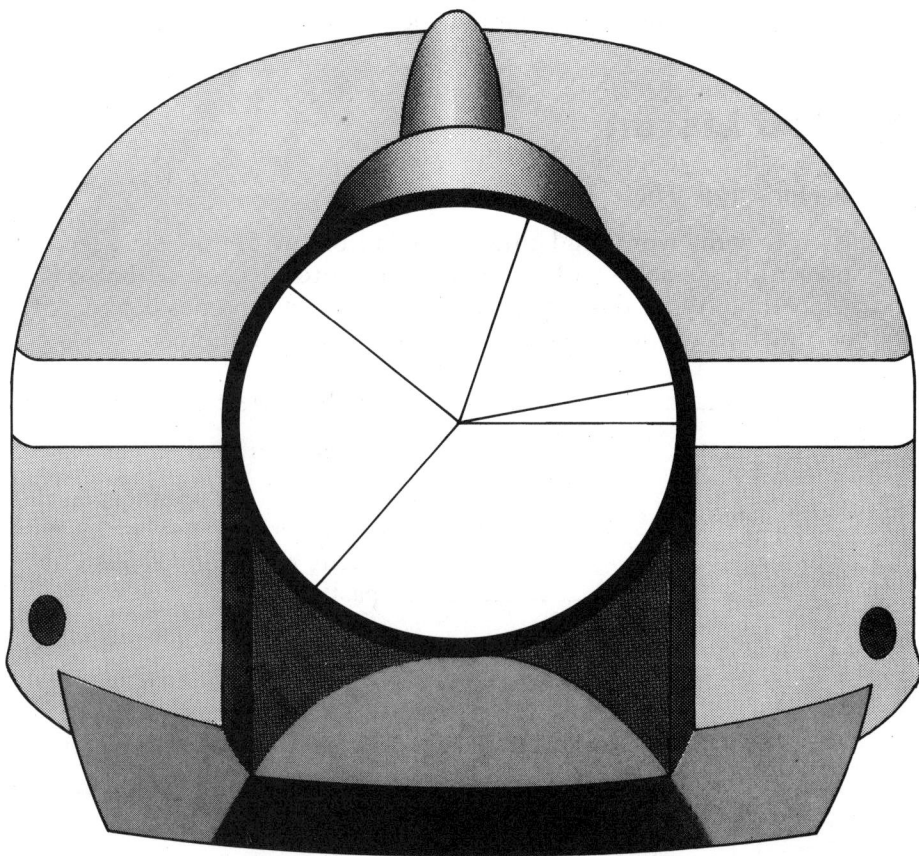

Before You Listen

1. *What's Your Opinion?*

What is the most important source of energy in the world today? What will be the most important source in the future? Why do you think so? Is your country dependent on energy supplies from other parts of the world? Do you think energy sources are an international or national issue? Why?

2. *Can You Predict?*

What are the different sources of energy? Can you estimate what percentage each source represents in the world's supply?

As You Listen

3. *Do You Know These Words?*

Listen to some words and phrases taken from part of the class lecture. You will hear each word or phrase in a sentence. You will also hear the spelling. Write down the word or phrase on the lines below. After you finish, find the meanings in the right-hand column.

1. _____   a. at the lowest position

2. _____   b. is the source of

                                                       c. material that produces heat or power and that comes from living things in the distant

3. _____   past

                                                       d. that is not much but that is

4. _____   all there is

                                                       e. total amount of available power which can be used to power machines, produce

5. _____   electricity, etc.

                                                       f. waste material, especially food wastes, and anything

6. _____   thrown away as useless

                                                       g. where power (for machines, etc.) comes from

7. _____

Now listen for these words and phrases in the recording. ●–●

4. *Were You Right?*

Look at the picture again as you listen to the tape. Were your predictions about the different sources of energy correct? Did you guess the percentage of each source? ●–●

5. *Identify the Focus*

Three sentences below have similar meanings. Put a check mark (✔) next to them. What's different about the remaining sentence? Now listen for the words that focus attention on the main idea in this part of the class presentation. ●–●

1. Five energy sources can be found in most countries around the world.

2. There are five various sources of energy on earth.

3. The world's energy supply comes from five sources.

4. What you have in the world is five different sorts of energy.

Which words did you actually hear? Can you think of another sentence with the same meaning?

6. *Making Notes: The Focus*

The focus of this summary of world energy sources can be written in note form this way:

world energy = 5 diff sorts

Which words are abbreviated? Which words were left out? What symbols were used?

Now using your own abbreviations and symbols, rewrite sentences two and three. Compare your notes with your classmates.

_____

_____

7. *Making Notes: The Supporting Details*

On the lines below take notes on the five sources of energy. Which source did the speaker leave out? Which three sources are related? ●–●

left out _____

Source   %

_____   _____

_____   _____

_____   _____

_____   _____

_____   _____

After You Listen

8. Can You Find Out?

1. Solar energy warms the earth, controls the weather cycles, and makes food crops possible. What percentage of world energy is solar energy? Why is solar energy not used more?

2. Invite a speaker from the local power company to your class. Find out about energy conservation programs in your city.

3. Some people are concerned about using up all fossil fuels. Interview as many people as you can. How many are worried about this issue? Why are they worried?

4. Draw a picture (or find one in a book or magazine) of a solar house. Explain how such a house uses solar energy.

5. Explain to the class how oil companies find oil. Illustrate your talk with diagrams or pictures.

9. Discussion

1. Nuclear energy is becoming more important to the world. What are the problems and the advantages of nuclear power? Do you think the problems are larger than the advantages or vice versa? Why? What is the feeling of most people in your country about nuclear energy?

2. How can the ordinary person save energy? Is it important to save energy? What are some public policies or programs that conserve energy? Are you personally worried that the world will use up all its energy sources? Why or why not?

UNIT 5

Population Movements

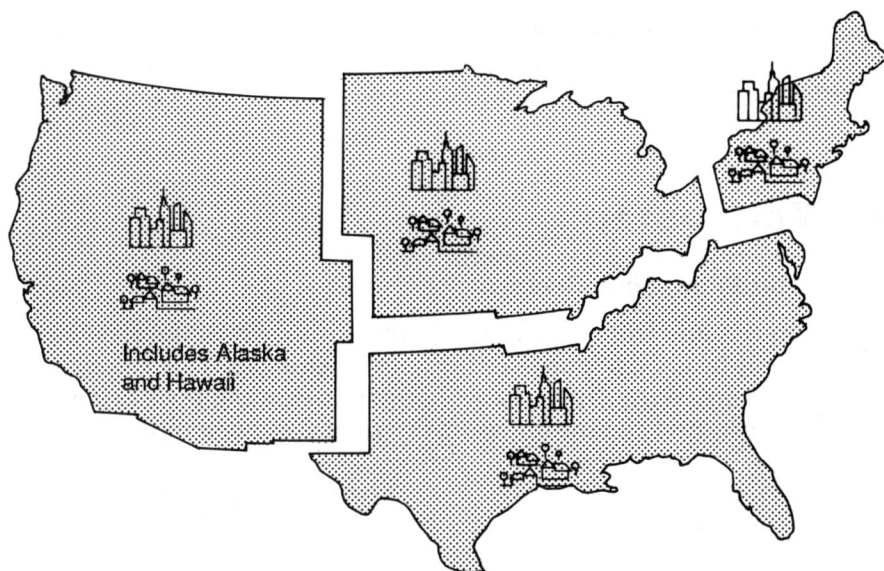

Includes Alaska and Hawaii

Before You Listen

1. What's Your Opinion?

Do you live in a city or in the country? Do you think one is better? Which one? With a partner, make a list of the advantages and disadvantages of city life and country life. Compare your lists with other classmates. Where do you want to live ten years from now? Thirty years from now? Why?

2. Can You Predict?

Look at the map of the U.S. The population in the four areas changed during the 1970s. Do you think more people moved to the cities or to the rural areas? Mark an increase (+) or a decrease (−) next to urban (city) and rural for all four areas.

As You Listen

3. Do You Know These Words?

Listen to some words and phrases taken from part of the class lecture. You will hear each word or phrase in a sentence. You will also hear the spelling. Write down the word or phrase on the lines below. After you finish, find the meanings in the right-hand column.

1. _____

2. _____

3. _____

4. _____

5. _____

6. _____

7. _____

8. _____

9. _____

a. areas that are in the countryside, away from cities

b. areas that have cities

c. became larger than

d. changes in human society

e. impressive

f. including everything

g. movements from one place to another

h. warm part of the country

i. with regard to

Now listen for these words and phrases in the recording.

4. Were You Right?

Listen to the excerpt about population shifts again. Were your predictions about which areas people are moving to accurate? [●-●]

5. Identify the Focus

Three sentences below have similar meanings. Put a check mark (✔) next to them. What is different about the remaining sentence? Now listen for the words that focus attention on the main idea in this part of the class presentation. [●-●]

1. From 1970 to 1980, rural areas in the United States surpassed urban areas in terms of the rate of population growth.

2. From 1970 to 1980, urban areas in the United States surpassed rural areas in terms of the rate of population growth.

3. In the decade of the 70s, the rate of population growth in the nonmetropolitan regions of the country exceeded the rate of growth in the metropolitan areas.

4. The rate of population growth in rural America was greater than that in urban America from 1970 to 1980.

Which words did you actually hear? Can you think of another sentence with the same meaning?

6. Making Notes: The Focus

The focus of this part of the class lecture can be written in note form this way:

1970–80 rural pop ↑ > urb pop

Which words are abbreviated? Which words were left out? What symbols are used?

Now using your own abbreviations and symbols, rewrite sentences three and four. Compare your notes with your classmates.

_____

_____

7. Making Notes: The Supporting Details

In the left-hand column are the areas of the country. In the right-hand column make notes about the change in population. ●─●

1. NE _____

2. NC _____

3. W _____

4. S _____

After You Listen

8. Can You Find Out?

1. Read the following excerpt from one person's letter about a recent move. Did the writer move to or from a city?

"Since I left LA, life is easier on me. I don't feel the stress of the clogged traffic, I don't have to deal with masses of people, live at such a fast pace or breathe polluted air. This is a beautiful area of the world: lots of water, hills, mountains, tall trees, and birds all over. As I look out my window, I see trees starting to bud. Signs of spring are all around. It's like always living in a beautiful landscape painting for me."

Can you imagine that you yourself might someday write a letter like this? Why? Do you agree or disagree with the writer's point of view? Why?

2. Go to the library at your school or to the public library. Ask the librarian to help you answer this question: "Where is the population moving in the 1980s?"

What reference book or books did you use? What book can give you the same type of information about your own country?

3. Where are people moving in your country? Use a map to explain to your classmates recent changes in population. Are these changes useful or good for the country?

4. The movie *Grapes of Wrath* is about the movement of many people in the United States in the 1930s. If you can, watch the movie. Where did people go? Why?

5. Interview ten people. Find out where they lived in 1970. Ask if they moved in the 1970s. If they moved, did they move from

city to city?

city to country?

country to country?

country to city?

Compare your answers with your classmates. Do your answers support the information in this unit?

9. Discussion

If you could choose any place in the world to live for one year, where would that be? Imagine that you are now living in that place. Write a short letter to a friend telling about your life in that place.

A Child's Motor Skills

From Mary M. Shirley, *The First Two Years*, Institute of Child Welfare Monograph No. 7. Minneapolis: University of Minnesota Press. Copyright © 1933, renewed 1961 by the University of Minnesota Press. Reprinted by permission.

Before You Listen

1. What's Your Opinion?

How old were you when you started walking? Was that early or late in your family? How do children learn the skills of sitting, crawling, walking, etc.? Can you "teach" a baby these skills? If so, how?

2. Can You Predict?

What motor skills do children learn from birth to 15 months of age? With a partner, make a list of the skills. Can you guess the average age a baby learns each skill?

As You Listen

3. Do You Know These Words?

Listen to some words and phrases taken from part of the class lecture. You will hear each word or phrase in a sentence. You will also hear the spelling. Write down the word or phrase on the lines below. After you finish, find the meanings in the right-hand column.

1. _____

2. _____

3. _____

4. _____

5. _____

6. _____

7. _____

8. _____

a. ability to use certain muscles in the body

b. before

c. correct and without mistakes

d. level of development

e. learning of more and more difficult movements

f. particular

g. way in which something usually happens

h. what comes first, second, etc.

Now listen for these words and phrases in the recording. 🔲

4. Were You Right?

Look at the pictures as you listen to the recording again. Were your predictions about when children learn different motor skills accurate? 🔲

5. Identify the Focus

Three sentences below have similar meanings. Put a check mark (✔) next to them. What is different about the remaining sentence? Now listen for the words that focus attention on the main idea in this part of the class presentation. 🔲

1. A child's motor skills are usually developed in a certain sequence.

2. Children's motor skills are usually learned in a predictable order.

3. The sequence in which a baby learns physical movements generally follows a certain order.

4. Children learn motor skills in many different sequences.

Which words did you actually hear? Can you think of another sentence with the same meaning?

6. Making Notes: The Focus

The focus of this part of the class lecture can be written in note form this way:

Chld's Motor Skills — devel'd certn seq

Which words are abbreviated? Which words were left out? What symbols are used?

Now using your own abbreviations and symbols, rewrite sentences two and three. Compare your notes with your classmates.

_____

_____

7. Making Notes: The Supporting Details

In the left column below, write down the skill a baby learns. In the right column, note the age the skill is learned. Use note forms wherever possible. 🔲

Skills	Age
_____	_____
_____	_____
_____	_____
_____	_____
_____	_____
_____	_____
_____	_____

After You Listen

8. Can You Find Out?

1. Arrange a trip to a nearby hospital. Observe the newborn babies. Listen to relatives and family friends talk about the babies. Write down some of the comments. Discuss your experience with your classmates.

2. Invite the school nurse to talk about early childhood development. What can or should a parent do with a child? What should an adult not do with a child?

3. Imagine you are a baby. Write a diary of your first 15 months of life. How did you learn one of the skills discussed in this unit? Who was there when you learned the skill? How did you feel? Read your "diary" to your classmates.

4. Read the following article, "Leave Policies: A World View." What is a "parental leave policy"? What do you think of this policy? Does your country have an official leave policy?

5. Conduct a telephone interview with the personnel manager of a large local company. Find out what the company's parental leave policy is. Report back to your classmates.

9. Discussion

1. Who should take care of a baby in the family? Just the mother? Both parents? Why do you think so?

2. Does your country have an official program for family planning and birth control? What is your personal opinion about planning the number of children in a family?

Leave Policies: A World View

By MARILYN MARKS
Times Staff Writer

Virtually all industrialized nations have public policies on parental leave and other issues faced by working parents. Some of these policies are summarized in a recent report by the Bureau of National Affairs, "Work and Family: A Changing Dynamic." A sampling is presented here:

- Sweden: Sweden allows a special pregnancy leave in addition to sick leave. A father may also take two weeks off with pay when his child is born. There is a "parents' allowance" of leave days so parents may stay home with sick children or visit a child's school. Parents of young children may work a six-hour day; they lose some pay but no other benefits. Day-care centers are run by municipalities, regulated by the central government, and financed through local taxes, parents' fees, and state subsidies from employer payroll deductions.
- Denmark: Either parent may take 10 weeks' leave after the regular maternity-leave period of 14 weeks. Parents receive 90 percent of pay, and adoptive parents are covered.
- France: Depending upon the type of employer, parents may take either unpaid leave or half-time leave for up to two years.
- Greece: A working mother and working father in a two-parent family may each take three months' unpaid leave. A single parent may take six months' leave. However, no more than 8 percent of the total work force may be on parental leave at one time, and time off is allocated on a first-come, first-served basis.
- Italy: Either parent may take up to six months of partially paid leave in the first year after a child's birth.
- Portugal: Either parent may take unpaid leave of between six months and two years during the child's first two years of life.
- Spain: Parents may cut back on work hours while caring for a young child. Unpaid parental leave may last as long as three years.

Despite these policies, Janet Norwood, commissioner of the U.S. Bureau of Labor Statistics, cautioned that "Europe is not doing as well as we all assume." Norwood noted that in many of these countries, working women remain the exception.

"How will Europe cope in the next few years, with an influx of women into the work force?" Norwood asked.

Completing High School

Before You Listen

1. What's Your Opinion?

In the U.S., everyone must go to school until the age of 16. Education is compulsory. How do you feel about forcing people to attend school? What are the good points and the bad points of compelling school attendance?

2. Can You Predict?

Between the 1950s and the 1980s, the percentage of adults who had completed high school rose in the U.S. Can you estimate the percentage of high school graduates in the adult population in 1981? 1975? 1970? 1960? 1950? By what year did a majority of adult Americans have a high school diploma?

As You Listen

3. Do You Know These Words?

Listen to some words and phrases taken from part of the class lecture. You will hear each word or phrase in a sentence. You will also hear the spelling. Write down the word or phrase on the lines below. After you finish, find the meanings in the right-hand column.

1. _____   a. a little

2. _____   b. collected numbers that show
                                   information

3. _____   c. finish

4. _____   d. greater number

5. _____   e. take as a fact or as true

6. _____   f. that has not always been true

7. _____   g. usual or ordinary

8. _____   h. went up

Now listen for these words and phrases in the recording. ▣

4. Were You Right?

Study the graph as you listen to the tape again. Were your estimates about the percentage of high school graduates accurate? ▣

5. Identify the Focus

Three sentences below have similar meanings. Put a check mark (✔)
next to them. What is different about the remaining sentence? Now
listen for the words that focus attention on the main idea in this part
of the class presentation. ▣▬●

1. From 1950 on, there has been a rise in the percentage of men and
   women who finish high school in the U.S.

2. Since 1950, the total percentage of graduates from American high
   schools has remained constant.

3. The percentage of adults who have completed high school in this
   country has increased since 1950.

4. The percentage of adults without high school diplomas has
   decreased from 1950 to 1981.

Which words did you actually hear? Can you think of another sentence with the same meaning?

6. Making Notes: The Focus

The focus of this part of the class lecture can be written in note form
this way:

> % adlts who hav compltd hs ↑ 1950–81

Which words are abbreviated? Which words were left out? What symbols are used?
   Now using your own abbreviations and symbols, rewrite sentences
one and four. Compare your notes with your classmates.

_____

_____

7. Making Notes: The Supporting Details

In the left column below, write the year mentioned by the speaker.
In the right column, jot down the percentage of adults who had completed high school by that year. ▣▬●

Year   Percentage

_____   _____

_____   _____

_____   _____

_____   _____

_____   _____

After You Listen

8. Can You Find Out?

1. In the magazine *Education Week* for September 7, 1981, there is an article titled "How the Public Views the Schools: Gallup 1981." There are seven charts in the article. Choose one and study it. Report the information to your classmates.

2. Go to a public library and find out if they have adult literacy classes. If they do, interview one of the teachers. Who are the students? How many are high school graduates? Who are the teachers? Why are the students now learning to read?

3. Imagine you cannot read. What problems would you have every day? For example, how would you order food in a restaurant? Would you be able to drive a car? How would you get to new places? Make a list of usual activities. Would they be easy or difficult without reading?

4. Spend a day in a high school with the students. What do students do all day? How similar or different was your own high school day? What was the most interesting part of the day?

5. Study the graph below. What is the graph about? What question did the researcher probably use? Ask ten people the same question. Compare your results.

9. Discussion

1. Do you think certain subjects in high school should be compulsory? Which subjects? Why? What subjects do you think will be the most valuable in 20 or 30 years? Why?

2. Why is reading for pleasure a good habit to develop? Do you read much in your free time? What kinds of books or magazines do you read? What is easiest for you to read in English?

The Major Problems Facing the Public Schools

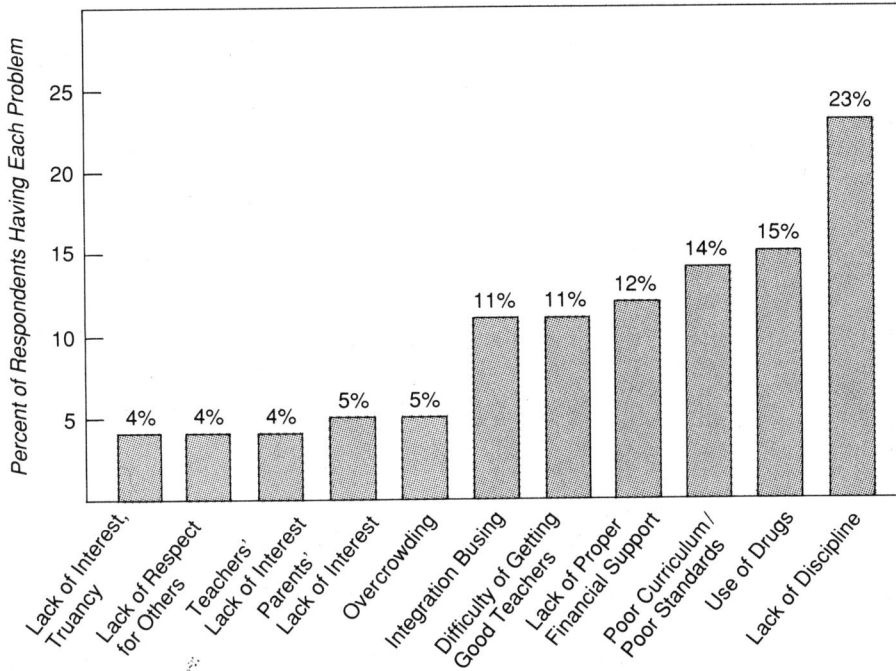

Reproduced from "How the Public Views the Schools: Gallup 1981" *Education Week*, September 7, 1981.

Large Families

1936 1978

Photo: Sharon Bode

Before You Listen

1. What's Your Opinion?

What is a large family? What are some of the advantages of a large family? What are the problems? How large is your family? What size is the best size for you? Why?

2. Can You Predict?

What has been the American attitude toward large families? What percentage of Americans would enjoy a family of more than four members? Estimate the percentages in 1936 and 1978.

As You Listen

3. Do You Know These Words?

Listen to some words and phrases taken from part of the class lecture. You will hear each word or phrase in a sentence. You will also hear the spelling. Write down the word or phrase on the lines below. After you finish, find the meanings in the right-hand column.

1. _____   a. a little bit
2. _____   b. approved
3. _____   c. change
4. _____   d. decrease

                                        e. facts helping to bring about
5. _____   a result
6. _____   f. feeling
7. _____   g. influence
8. _____   h. quick

Now listen for these words and phrases in the recording. [▣]

4. Were You Right?

Look at the graph as you listen again to the tape. Were your estimates about how many people would like a family of four or more correct? [▣]

5. Identify the Focus

Three sentences below have similar meanings. Put a check mark (✔) next to them. What is different about the remaining sentence? Now listen for the words that focus attention on the main idea in this part of the class presentation. 【●-●】

1. Feelings about having a large family have remained about the same in the U.S.

2. Over the years people in this country have felt differently about having large families.

3. People's attitudes in favor of big families have gone up and down.

4. There's been a general fluctuation of attitude toward large families in the U.S.

Which words did you actually hear? Can you think of another sentence with the same meaning?

6. Making Notes: The Focus

The focus of this part of the class lecture can be written in note form this way:

US attit ↗↘ re: larg fam

Which words are abbreviated? Which words were left out? What symbols are used?

Now using your own abbreviations and symbols, rewrite sentences two and three. Compare your notes with your classmates.

_____

_____

7. Making Notes: The Supporting Details

In the left-hand column below, write down the years the speaker mentions. In the right-hand column, write the percentage of Americans who wanted a large family in that year. 【●-●】

Year	*Percentage*
_____	_____
_____	_____
_____	_____
_____	_____
_____	_____
_____	_____
_____	_____

After You Listen

8. Can You Find Out?

1. Study the pattern of the graph. Notice what year the highest point was. Why do you think people wanted more children that year? When was the largest change? What was the direction of the change? In your opinion, what might be some reasons for the changes in direction?

2. Go to the library and find the most recent information on this question: "What happens to the line after 1978?" Compare the U.S. statistics with similar information about your own country. Are the patterns similar or different? Report back to your class.

3. Look at the summary of 1980 survey information below. What question did the interviewer ask? Do you agree with the majority opinion? What would your answer be? Why? Ask ten people the same question. Put your answers together with your classmates' answers. Did you get the same results?

Ideal Family Size

One	3%
Two	51
Three	21
Four	12
Five	2
Six or more	2
None	1
Don't know	8

Interviewing Date: 3/7–10/80
Survey #150-G

4. Invite a speaker from a community organization, e.g., Planned Parenthood, to talk about population issues. What are some of the programs around the world to help people plan the size of their families?

5. See the movie *Cheaper by the Dozen*. What is the meaning of the title? Would you be happy in such a family? Why or why not?

9. *Discussion*

1. What is a family? What are the responsibilities, if any, of family members to each other? In your society, what happens to older members of the family when they can't care for themselves? How do you feel about taking care of other people in your family?

2. In your own opinion, what are the advantages and disadvantages of having a family with only one or two children? What are the advantages and disadvantages of having more than two children? For your own family, which would you prefer?

UNIT 9

A Cracker House

Reprinted by permission of Florida State Archives

Before You Listen

1. What's Your Opinion?

What do houses in your country look like? Is there a typical or traditional house style? What is it made of? Is the weather related to the design of the house? What's the best thing about living in that kind of house? What's the worst thing?

2. Can You Predict?

Look at the picture of the house. What kind of weather do you think this house is made for? Why is the house above the ground? What is the purpose of the porch around the house? Where in the United States do you think you might find this kind of house? Why?

As You Listen

3. Do You Know These Words?

Listen to some words and phrases taken from part of the class lecture. You will hear each word or phrase in a sentence. You will also hear the spelling. Write down the word or phrase on the lines below. After you finish, find the meanings in the right-hand column.

1. _____   a. a change (of a house)

2. _____   b. an example

3. _____   c. a person who was born in the South

4. _____   d. a space between the roof and the ceiling of a house

5. _____   e. parts

6. _____   f. the geography and weather of a place

7. _____   g. the shape or design of something, e.g., a house

8. _____   h. the use or purpose of something, e.g., a house

Now listen for these words and phrases in the recording.

4. Were You Right?

Look at the house again as you listen to the teacher on the tape talk about it. Did you guess where you can find such a house and why? ●-●

5. Identify the Focus

Three sentences below have similar meanings. Put a check mark (✔) next to them. What's different about the remaining sentence? Now listen for the words that focus attention on the main idea in this part of the class presentation. ●-●

1. Crackers have developed a kind of architecture that exemplifies the concept that form follows function.

2. First crackers built formal houses, then functional houses.

3. The design of a cracker house matches the use of the house.

4. When you look at a cracker house, you can see that form and function are very closely related.

Which words did you actually hear? Can you think of another sentence with the same meaning?

6. Making Notes: The Focus

The focus of this part of the class lecture can be written in note form this way:

> crackrs hav develpd architctr: form follows fnctn

Which words are abbreviated? Which words were left out? What symbols are used?

Now using your own abbreviations and symbols, rewrite sentences three and four. Compare your notes with your classmates.

_____

_____

7. Making Notes: The Supporting Details

In the left-hand column below, write down the different parts of the house as you hear them mentioned. In the right column, note the function as explained by the speaker. ●-●

Form	Function
_____	_____
_____	_____
_____	_____
_____	_____
_____	_____
_____	_____

After You Listen

8. Can You Find Out?

1. Find a picture (or draw one) of a typical house from your city or country. Describe the form and function of the house to your classmates. What kind of weather is the house made for?

2. Invite a teacher in the urban planning or architecture department to speak to your class. Ask the speaker to give a slide lecture presentation about housing in the local area.

3. At this time architects are designing houses of the future. Some will be for use under the sea or out in space. Find or create an example of a future house. What forms and functions will this (your) house have?

4. You have just invented a new technology. It will change how we live at home. What is your invention? How will people use it? Explain your idea to a group of classmates who are pretending to be investors. They will give you money if they like your idea.

5. Go to the library and find a 1987 *Wall Street Journal* article by Alix M. Freedman titled "Form Mimics Function in New Product Design." Give a report to the class on the different products in the article.

9. Discussion

1. What kind of building do you live in now? Is it a house? Is it an apartment? Is it a dorm? What is the general style of the building? Do you like the design? Is it practical? What are some of the things you like best about it? Are there things you don't like about

it? If you were designing a similar building, what changes would you make?

2. The kind of place a person lives in clearly has an effect on how that person feels and acts. Make a list of a few different places you could now be living in that exist in your area. What effect would each place have on your life? Why? If you could freely choose, which place would you prefer to live in? Why?

Immigration to Hawaii

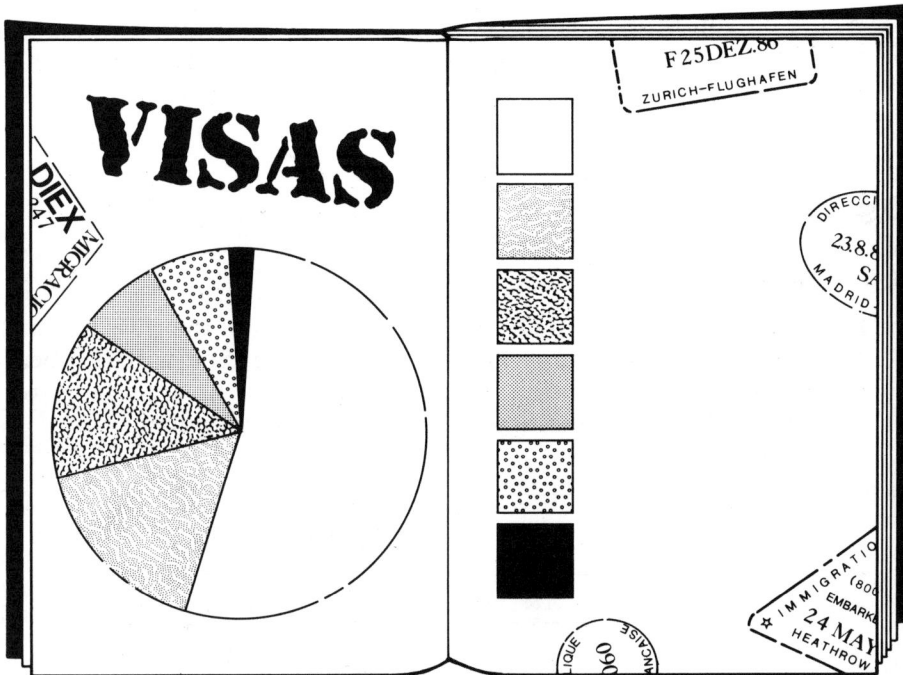

Before You Listen

1. What's Your Opinion?

What are some of the changes people go through when they emigrate from one country to another? With a partner, make a list of the reasons. What are the positive changes? What are the negative changes? What are some differences between adult immigrants and children who are immigrants?

2. Can You Predict?

Try to remember all you've heard about Hawaii and its racial mix. Where do you think most of Hawaii's immigrants came from in the past? Why? During the decade of the 70s, where do you think they came from? Why?

As You Listen

3. Do You Know These Words?

Listen to some words and phrases taken from part of the class lecture. You will hear each word or phrase in a sentence. You will also hear the spelling. Write down the word or phrase on the lines below. After you finish, find the meanings in the right-hand column.

1. _____

2. _____

3. _____

4. _____

5. _____

6. _____

7. _____

8. _____

a. because

b. directed by the state government

c. general

d. group

e. group that includes all other small groups

f. instead of

g. people from other countries who have come to the U.S. to live and whose native language is not English

h. unusual

i. what might these statistics
mean or why are these
9. _____   statistics important

Now listen for these words and phrases in the recording. [●–●]

4. Were You Right?

Look at the chart again as you listen to the tape. Were your predictions about the immigrants to Hawaii correct? [●–●]

5. Identify the Focus

Three sentences below have similar meanings. Put a check mark (✔)
next to them. What's different about the remaining sentence? Now
listen for the words that focus attention on the main idea in this part
of the class presentation. [●–●]

1. All other states have special problems in education similar to
   Hawaii's.

2. Hawaii has a number of special problems in the area of education.

3. Hawaiian education has some problems that educational systems
   in other states don't share.

4. Some of the problems in Hawaiian public education are different
   from problems in other state school systems.

Which words did you actually hear? Can you think of another sentence with the same meaning?

6. Making Notes: The Focus

The focus of this part of the class lecture can be written in note form
this way:

HI has # spec probs in educa'n

Which words are abbreviated? Which words were left out? What symbols are used?
   Now using your own abbreviations and symbols, rewrite sentences
three and four. Compare your notes with your classmates.

_____

_____

7. Making Notes: The Supporting Details

Use the outline below to make notes about the information about education in Hawaii. 🔲●▪●

HI has spec probs in educ

1. sys at state lev not city/cnty
2. largest % of non-nat spkg immig/pop.
3. larg % attnd priv not pub school

e.g. look @ 70's

1. 6 grps

   a. Phil   _____

   b.   _____

   c.   _____

   d.   _____

   e.   _____

   f.   _____

2. _____?

After You Listen

8. Can You Find Out?

1. How many people from your country have immigrated to the U.S. in the last ten years? Ask the librarian to help you find the answer. What percentage of all immigrants does your country represent? What are some of the reasons people come to the U.S. from your country?

2. Invite a speaker to talk to your class about the sanctuary movement in the U.S. Who are the immigrants? Who is helping them? Why?

3. If you have a video cassette recorder, or if you can borrow one, see the movie *Moscow on the Hudson.* Who are the immigrants in the movie? Why did they leave home? What problems did they have? What good experiences did they have?

4. Choose another state that you are interested in. Go to the library and find out about its recent immigrants. How is it similar to Hawaii?

5. Imagine that you are a salesperson from your country. You want people to immigrate there. What reasons can you give to help someone choose it? What advice can you give to the new immigrants about living in their new home?

9. Discussion

1. Does your home country accept immigrants? What is the government policy? How do you, personally, feel about the policy? Have many people immigrated there in the past decade? Where are they from? Why have they moved?

2. Which do you think is better for new immigrants:
   a. totally becoming part of the new culture
   b. keeping much or most of the old culture
   Is your answer the same for the short run (i.e., a few years) and for the long run (many years or a lifetime)?

UNIT 11

The Demographic Transition

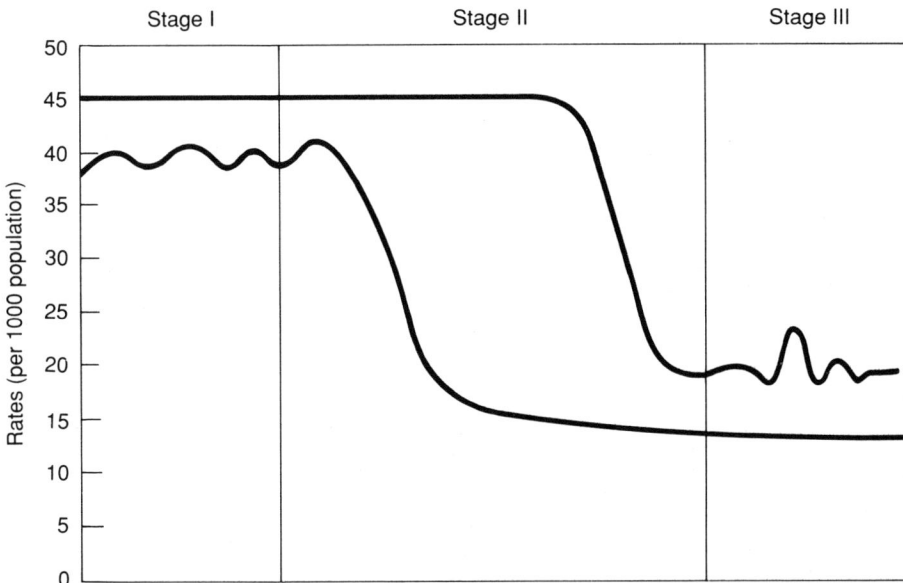

Before You Listen

1. What's Your Opinion?

What do you think the term *birth rate* means? How about *death rate*? Why is the birth rate high or low in a country? Why is the death rate high or low? Does the government of your country have a program or policy to increase or decrease the number of births or deaths?

2. Can You Predict?

There is a general pattern for birth rates and death rates in a developing country. What is the pattern at the beginning? in the middle? after a country is very developed? What are the reasons for the changes?

As You Listen

3. Do You Know These Words?

Listen to some words and phrases taken from part of the class lecture. You will hear each word or phrase in a sentence. You will also hear the spelling. Write down the word or phrase on the lines below. After you finish, find the meanings in the right-hand column.

1. _____   a. a change

b. a country is changing from a
simple society to a more
2. _____   complex society

3. _____   c. continue to live

d. people who study the size,
growth, statistics, and so on
4. _____   of human populations

5. _____   e. suddenly and clearly

f. the number of babies born
6. _____   (usually) per 1000 people

g. the number of people who die
7. _____   (usually) per 1000 people

h. the relationship of the birth
8. _____   rate to the death rate

i. usual medical care and
9. _____   knowledge

Now listen for these words and phrases in the recording. `●-●`

4. *Were You Right?*

Look at the graph again as you listen to the tape. Were your predictions about the pattern of births and deaths accurate? `●-●`

5. *Identify the Focus*

Three sentences below have similar meanings. Put a check mark (✔) next to them. What's different about the remaining sentence? Now listen for the words that focus attention on the main idea in this part of the class presentation. `●-●`

1. All countries change their birth rates and death rates in the same way.

2. Most countries have similar changes of birth rates and death rates as they develop.

3. The demographic pattern is pretty predictable in developing nations.

4. When countries become more modern, there is a usual pattern of change in how many babies are born and how many people die.

Which words did you actually hear? Can you think of another sentence with the same meaning?

6. *Making Notes: The Focus*

The focus of this part of the class lecture can be written in note form this way:

> demogra'c transi'n predic'bl in develg nat'ns

Which words are abbreviated? Which words were left out?
   Now using your own abbreviations and symbols, rewrite sentences two and four. Compare your notes with your classmates.

_____

_____

7. *Making Notes: The Supporting Details*

As you listen to the teacher talk about the demographic pattern, take down the information that explains the graph on the first page of this unit. Use note form. `●-●`

def. demogrphrs = _____

_____

1st stage _____

Why? _____

2nd stage _____

Why? _____

3rd stage _____

Why? _____

After You Listen

8. Can You Find Out?

1. What is the "baby boom" in the United States? When did it start? Why is it important?

2. Many women in the U.S. go to the hospital to have their babies. Other women go to a "birthing center." If there is a birthing center in your city, find out if you can go and visit the center. Report back to the class on the difference between a hospital and a birthing center.

3. Buy or borrow an almanac and bring it to class. What kind of demographic information is in an almanac?

4. Interview the marketing teacher in the business department. How do businesses use demographic information to sell goods and services? How important is the "baby boom" to businesses?

5. Study the graph below. Based on the information in the recording, describe the graph. What stage in the demographic transition is shown? What is the relationship of the birth rate and the death rate? What other information is in the graph? Give a one- to two-minute analysis of the graph to the class.

9. Discussion

1. In terms of demographics, which of the three stages would you consider your home country to be in at the present time? Why? How long has it been at its present stage? Do you think its present stage is likely to continue for the next few years or will it possibly change? Why?

Components of Population Change: 1955 to 1981

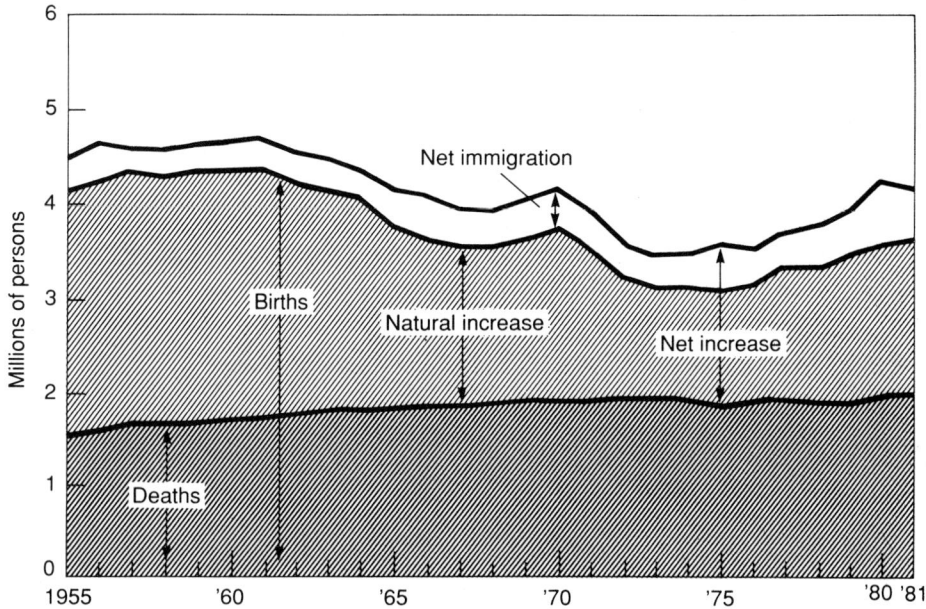

Chart prepared by U.S. Bureau of the Census.

2. Certain informal activities often accompany births in the U.S. For example, new parents often send out cards announcing the arrival of a baby. Female friends of a new mother may give the baby gifts at a party called a baby shower. The color pink is used if the baby is a girl. Blue is used if the baby is a boy. A new father may hand out cigars to his friends and business associates. What activities accompany births in your home country? Are specific colors used?

The Advantages of Exporting

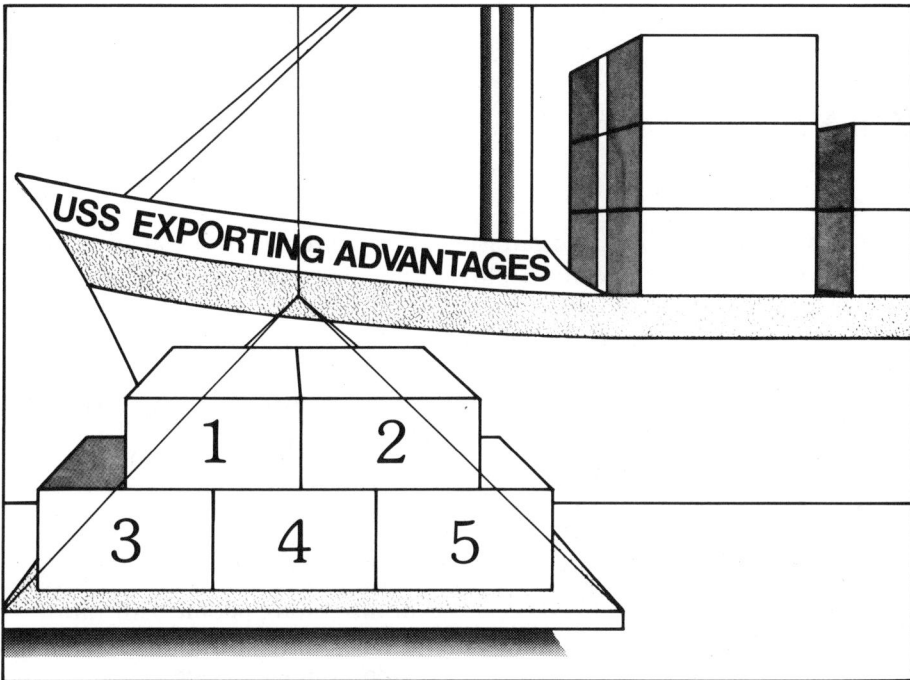

Before You Listen

1. What's Your Opinion?

What products do you know of that your country exports to other countries? Are the export companies generally large or small? How important is international trade to your country? Does a company have to be very large to be an international trader?

2. Can You Predict?

Why would a small company enter the exporting business? What are some advantages of exporting for a small business?

As You Listen

3. Do You Know These Words?

Listen to some words and phrases taken from part of the class lecture. You will hear each word or phrase in a sentence. You will also hear the spelling. Write down the word or phrase on the lines below. After you finish, find the meanings in the right-hand column.

1. _____

a. a company getting larger

b. a list that shows when a company will make and sell a product

2. _____

3. _____

c. good points

d. how long people will know and buy a company's products/services

4. _____

e. materials/people that a company uses to make its products

5. _____

f. new places to sell a company's products or services

6. _____

g. people who buy a company's products or services

7. _____

h. repeat the main points without any of the details

8. _____

9. _____   i. the people who work in a
                                   company

Now listen for these words and phrases in the recording. $\boxed{\bullet\text{-}\bullet}$

4. Were You Right?

Look at the picture again as you listen to the tape. Were your predictions accurate about the advantages of exporting for a small business? $\boxed{\bullet\text{-}\bullet}$

5. Identify the Focus

Three sentences below have similar meanings. Put a check mark (ν)
next to them. What's different about the remaining sentence? Now
listen for the words that focus attention on the main idea in this part
of the class presentation. $\boxed{\bullet\text{-}\bullet}$

1. And now I'd like to summarize some of the advantages for small
   businesses getting into the export business.

2. At this point, I'll pull together the main reasons exporting is a
   good idea for small companies.

3. Next I'd like to go into a little more detail about the advantages
   of international trade for small businesses.

4. So the main reasons it's useful for a company to think about
   exporting can be summed up this way.

Which words did you actually hear? Can you think of another sentence with the same meaning?

6. Making Notes: The Focus

The focus of this part of the class lecture can be written in note form
this way:

          sum advan of exprtg fr sm bus

Which words are abbreviated? Which words were left out? What symbols are used?
   Now using your own abbreviations and symbols, rewrite sentences
two and four. Compare your notes with your classmates.

_____

_____

7. Making Notes: The Supporting Details

In the left-hand column, the speaker's main points are stated as single words. As you listen again to the summary, take notes on each point. Compare your notes with your classmates. [●-●]

1. mkts _____

_____

2. custmrs _____

_____

3. prod life _____

_____

4. corp. growth _____

_____

5. planning _____

_____

After You Listen

8. Can You Find Out?

1. Find a small export business in your community. Interview the owner or manager. Why did the company choose to export its product or service? What were the advantages for that business? (The Chamber of Commerce might be helpful to you.)

2. The speaker summarized five advantages. Choose a company or a product that is a good example of one of the advantages. Present a short history of the company to the class.

3. You work for a small company. You believe that the company product is perfect for exporting to another country. Persuade the president of the company to export the product. The product can be real or imaginary.

4. What are the main exports from your country? What are the main imports to your country? Use the library to locate the most recent statistics to answer this question. Report back to the class.

5. Take one of the business concepts from the note-taking exercise. For example, you could choose the life cycle of a product. Explain, with charts, graphs, etc., the meaning of the concept in a class presentation.

6. Study the visual information below. With a partner, decide what each symbol means. Then summarize the information in words for the class.

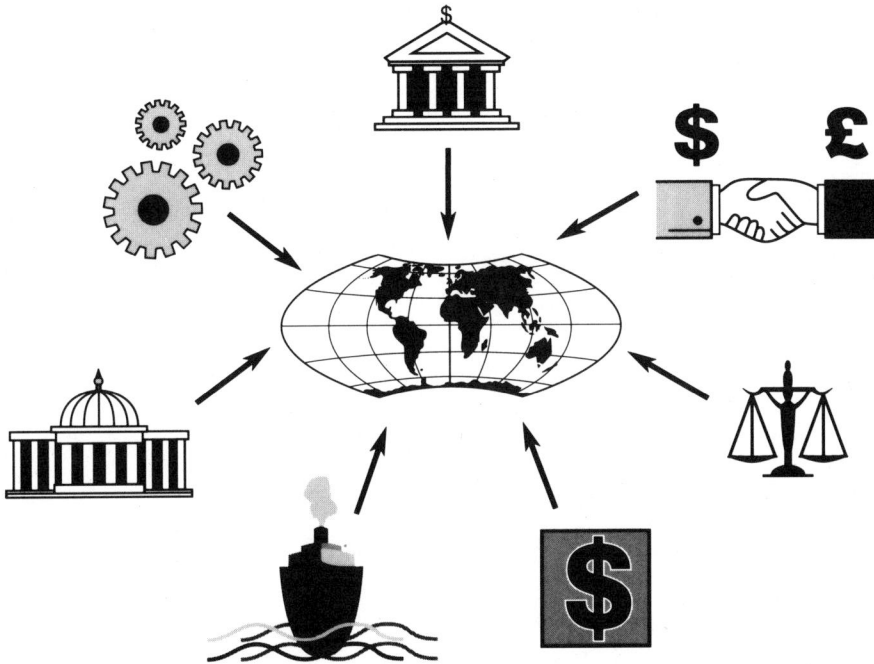

9. Discussion

1. Some countries with more or less unrestricted trade policies allow others to export goods into their markets. Some countries with restricted trade policies allow relatively few outside products in. Try to think of some countries that allow "free trade" and try to think of some that don't. Why do you think those countries have those policies? Generally, what are the advantages and disadvantages for countries with free trade? How about for those that don't have free trade? What effect do you think each policy has on the general world economy? How about on international relations?

2. If you were completely free to choose, would you prefer to have a career in business or would you prefer something else? Why do you feel that way? What would your family and friends think of that career choice?

Government Expenditures

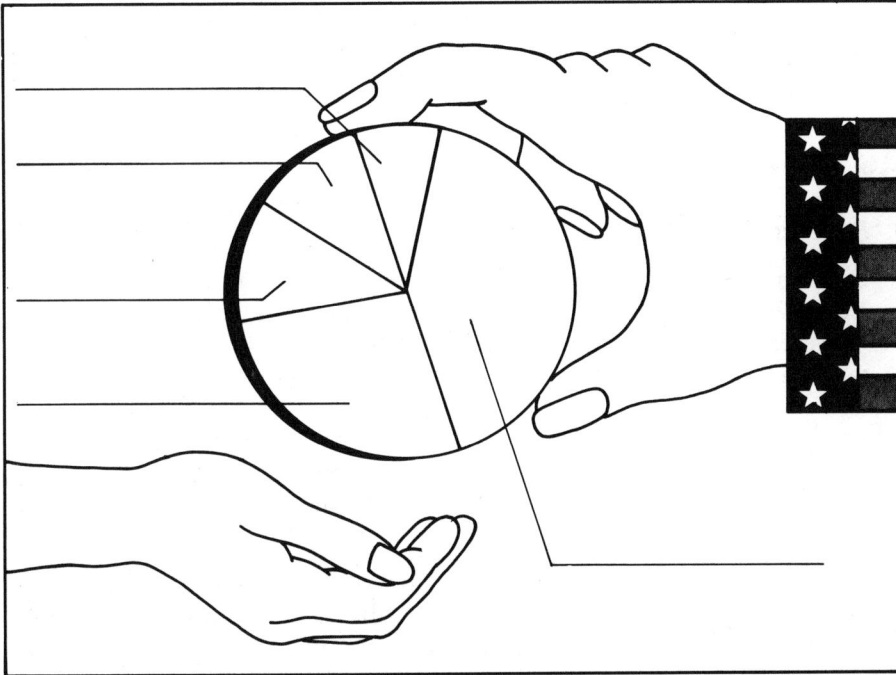

Before You Listen

1. What's Your Opinion?

In your family, who receives money for their work? Who decides how to spend that money? Does your family have a budget? Do you follow a strict budget? What are the categories in your budget? What is the largest category? Do you think a budget is a good idea? Why?

2. Can You Predict?

What do governments budget money for? Make a list of possible government expenditures. Discuss your list with other students. Combine your items into five or so main groups. What percentage of government dollars is spent in each area?

As You Listen

3. Do You Know These Words?

Listen to some words and phrases taken from part of the class lecture. You will hear each word or phrase in a sentence. You will also hear the spelling. Write down the word or phrase on the lines below. After you finish, find the meanings in the right-hand column.

1. _____

a. cause the amount of money being taken in and the amount of money being spent to be equal

2. _____

b. keeping the U.S. safe from harm by paying for the army, the navy, and so on

3. _____

c. money given by the U.S. government to cities, states, countries, and so on

4. _____

d. money given by the U.S. government to individual people

5. _____

e. money spent by the U.S. government

6. _____

f. money that must be paid (in this case, by the U.S. government) to borrow money

7. _____

g. reduce the amount of money being spent

h. the government's plan, being used now, which tells how much money is being taken in and how it is being spent

8. _____

i. the group which is made up of several small unnamed expenses

9. _____

j. the present national government

10. _____

Now listen for these words and phrases in the recording.

4. Were You Right?

Look at the graph again as you listen to the student's comments on the budget. Were your predictions about the percentages for each category correct?

5. Identify the Focus

Three sentences below have similar meanings. Put a check mark (✔) next to them. What's different about the remaining sentence? Now listen for the words that focus attention on the main idea in this part of the class presentation.

1. Right now the government budgets tax dollars for five kinds of expenses.

2. There are five categories of government expenditures in the current budget.

3. There are five categories of government revenues in the current budget.

4. The national budget reveals five main categories of expenditures.

Which words did you actually hear? Can you think of another sentence with the same meaning?

6. Making Notes: The Focus

The focus of this part of the class lecture can be written in note form this way:

5 categ of expenditr in curr budgt

Which words are abbreviated? Which words were left out? What symbols are used?

Now using your own abbreviations and symbols, rewrite sentences one and four. Compare your notes with your classmates.

_____

_____

7. Making Notes: The Supporting Details

In the left-hand column, write down the five categories of expenditures mentioned by the speaker. In the right-hand column, write down the percentage of the budget for each category. 〔●■●〕

_____   _____

_____   _____

_____   _____

_____   _____

_____   _____

What is the speaker's reason for telling these statistics to the professor (and her class)? Use your own note forms to write down the speaker's two questions.

_____

_____

_____

_____

After You Listen

8. Can You Find Out?

1. Talk to an economics teacher. Find out more details about the federal budget. Who does the government pay directly? What expenses does the federal government share with cities and states? What is the actual dollar amount of the budget?

2. Imagine that a close friend of yours is planning to study in the U.S. Your friend has asked you to make a one-year budget. With a partner, make a list of expenses for one year.

3. What does your country's budget look like? Compare the major categories with the U.S. budget in this unit. How does your government raise money for its expenditures? Use a chart or graph to give a class report.

4. Interview ten tax-paying adults. Find out how they feel about the different categories of government spending. Do they believe the budget should be balanced? Would they agree to increase taxes to balance the budget? Summarize your results for the other students.

9. Discussion

1. What should a national government spend tax money for? What should private citizens pay for? What does the government spend too much for or too little for? How would you divide the pie of government tax dollars?

2. Disposable income is the amount of money people have after they pay for food, housing, clothing, and other necessary expenses. How do you spend most of your disposable income? Has this changed in the last year or so? How are your spending habits similar to those of your friends? How are they different?

Ecosystems

Solar Energy

CO_2 and H_2O

Green plants
(producers)

Nutrient Pool

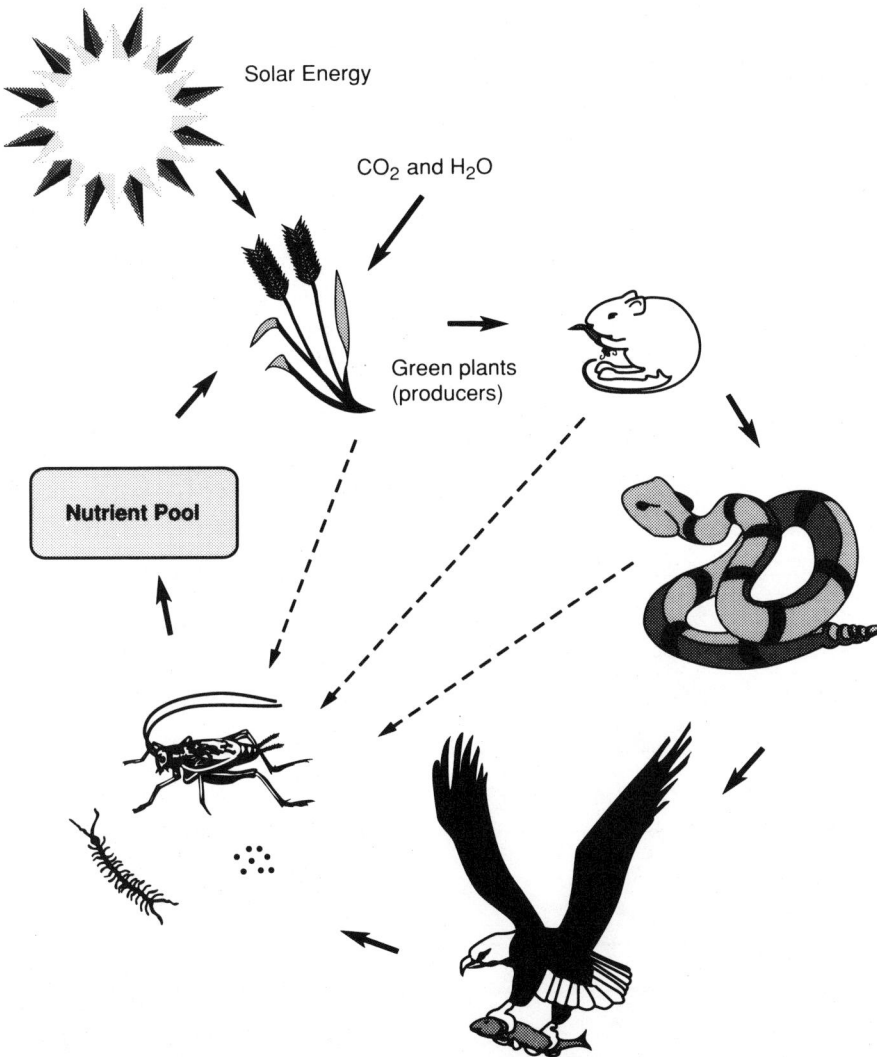

From *Physical Science*, 2/E, by Jonathan Turk and Amos Turk © 1981 by Holt, Rinehart
and Winston, Inc. Reprinted by permission of the publisher.

Before You Listen

1. What's Your Opinion?

Often when people build a city, the animals and plants in that area go away. Some people worry about disappearing animals and plants. They also think about the quality of the air and water. They think there is a delicate balance among all living things. Other people don't worry about these issues at all. What do you think?

2. Can You Predict?

Without looking at a dictionary, what do you think the word "ecosystem" means? Can you describe what takes place in an ecosystem?

As You Listen

3. Do You Know These Words?

Listen to some words and phrases taken from part of the class lecture. You will hear each word or phrase in a sentence. You will also hear the spelling. Write down the word or phrase on the lines below. After you finish, find the meanings in the right-hand column.

1. _____

2. _____

3. _____

4. _____

5. _____

6. _____

7. _____

8. _____

9. _____

a. a group of related parts that are connected to each other in a way that makes one depend on the other

b. allow and make possible

c. animals which eat grass and plants

d. animals which eat meat

e. an interrelated group

f. a shared supply of food that provides for life and growth

g. closely corresponding to or almost the same in purpose, position, etc.

h. comprised of or including

i. living and then dying and then living and then dying, etc.

10. _____ j. strange and unusual

k. the remains of animals or plants after decomposition or rotting

11. _____

Now listen for these words and phrases in the recording. ▣

4. Were You Right?

Look at the ecosystem in the picture again as you listen to the teacher describe it. Was your definition close to the one you heard? Was your description accurate? ▣

5. Identify the Focus

Three sentences below have similar meanings. Put a check mark (✔) next to them. What's different about the remaining sentence? Now listen for the words that focus attention on the main idea in this part of the class presentation. ▣

1. A community of animals, plants, and bacteria forms an unrelated system called an ecosystem.

2. A group of animals, plants, and bacteria forming an interconnected system is called an ecosystem.

3. An ecosystem is an interrelated system made up of a community of animals, plants, and bacteria.

4. Ecosystem describes the interrelationships of a community of animals, plants, and bacteria.

Which words did you actually hear? Can you think of another sentence with the same meaning?

6. Making Notes: The Focus

The focus of this part of the class lecture can be written in note form this way:

ecosys = interrelated sys = commty of anim/plants/bact

Which words are abbreviated? Which words were left out?

Now using your own abbreviations and symbols, rewrite sentences two and four. Compare your notes with your classmates.

_____

_____

7. Making Notes: The Supporting Details

Read the notes below. With a partner or in a group, decide what each one means. Then listen again to the description of the ecosystem. Are the notes in the "correct" order? If not, renumber them in the order you hear on the tape. Are all of them "true"? If not, put an F for false next to the number. ▐●–●▌

1. strtg pt the pool of nutrnts = minerals fr plants

2. plant-eatg anim = herbivore

3. exotc anim = carn = pandas, koalas

4. meat-eatg anim (carnivores) eat herb.

5. anim + plants — die — decay organisms — nutrients

6. sm meat-eatr eat othr meat eatr

Compare the notes with the picture. What part of the explanation did the teacher leave out? Write it in note form below.

After You Listen

8. Can You Find Out?

1. Ask the geology, geography, or biology teacher to take your class on a field trip. Find out as much as you can about the natural ecosystem of the area you live in.

2. Is there danger to an ecosystem someplace in your own country? What is the danger? Where does it come from? Use maps, pictures, and any other visual material to explain this issue to the class.

3. What was the great "dust bowl" of the 1930s in the United States? What happened to the ecology of the "dust bowl" area? If you can, find old pictures or news films about this period of time from the library. Did the "dust bowl" have to happen?

4. Study the picture below of a simple forest ecosystem. Use the picture to explain what an ecosystem is.

9. Discussion

1. What experiences have you had living in a natural environment? Do you go, or have you ever gone, camping or hiking? Do you enjoy outdoor activities or do you prefer activities in the city more? Is direct contact with nature important to you? Why or why not?

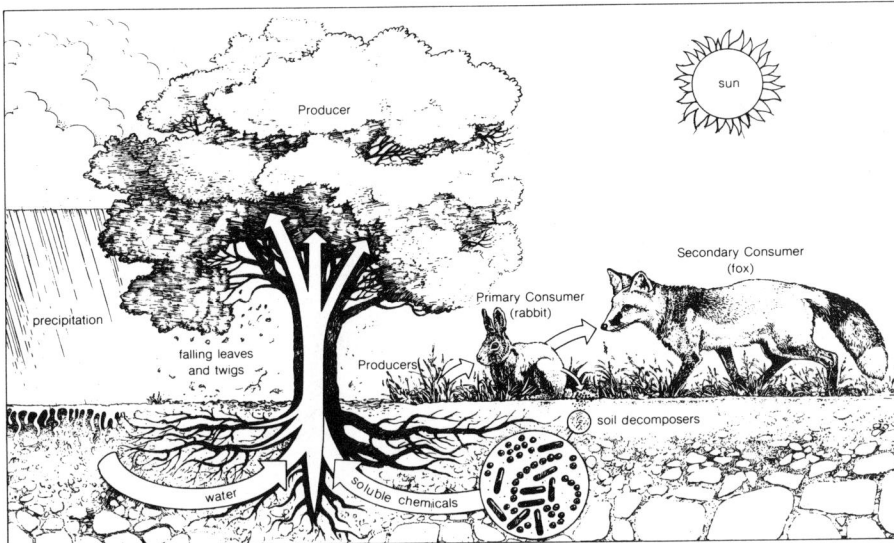

From *Living in the Environment*, Third Edition, by G. Tyler Miller, Jr. © 1982 by Wadsworth, Inc. Reprinted by permission of the publisher.

2. Do you think pollution is an important issue? What kinds of pollution are most common where you are from? Are there public programs to reduce pollution? What can individuals do about pollution? Are you, yourself, doing any of those things?

International Student Survey

Adjusting to College Life

Of the choices below, which do you expect will be the hardest part of adjusting to college?

Adjustment problem	Me	Most Students
becomg a critcl & indep thinkr		
budgtg time		
decidg whethr or how much to get involvd in camp activ		
earng satis grades		
mtg & kng othr studs		
mtg finan expen		
selectg field of study &/or career		
studyg efficly		

Before You Listen

1. What's Your Opinion?

Students have to adjust themselves to new conditions when they go to a college or a university. To be successful they often have to change the way they do things, and making those changes can sometimes cause adjustment problems. What are some of the adjustments that students have to make when they go to college? After becoming a college student, what did you have to do differently as compared to the time before you were a college student? Did you expect those changes? Was it easy or was it difficult for you to make those changes?

2. Can You Predict?

Look at the list of possible adjustments that college students might have to make. With a partner, try to decide what each item means. Then you, yourself, answer the survey question. Next guess how a group of international students actually answered the question.

As You Listen

3. Do You Know These Words?

Listen to some words and phrases taken from part of the class lecture. You will hear each word or phrase in a sentence. You will also hear the spelling. Write down the word or phrase on the lines below. After you finish, find the meanings in the right-hand column.

1. _____

   a. an information system in many libraries

   b. a person who can form opinions or make decisions without help from others

2. _____

   c. a person who thinks carefully before forming an opinion or before accepting the opinions of others

3. _____

   d. a printed paper that has places to write answers to questions and which can show people's opinions

4. _____

5. _____

6. _____

7. _____

8. _____

9. _____

10. _____

11. _____

e. being able to pay for every-thing that is needed

f. divisions; groups

g. participate, or take part, in things that are done for inter-est or education at a school

h. planning how to use one's time well and following that plan

i. problems that people have which are related to getting accustomed to living in a new or foreign place

j. using one's study time well and without wasting time

k. written to show the most important, the next impor-tant, and so on

Now listen for these words and phrases in the recording. ●▬●

4. Were You Right?

Listen to the teacher reporting the results of the survey again. Did you guess correctly what would be the number-one problem for the group of international students? ●▬●

5. Identify the Focus

Three sentences below have similar meanings. Put a check mark (✔) next to them. What's different about the remaining sentence? Now listen for the words that focus attention on the main idea in this part of the class presentation. ●▬●

1. Foreign students evaluate possible problems with study in the U.S.

2. International students rank the adjustment problems to American study.

3. Problems for international students concern many American colleges.

4. The survey reveals the ranking of adjustments to study in America by a group of international students.

Which words did you actually hear? Can you think of another sen-tence with the same meaning?

6. Making Notes: The Focus

The focus of this part of the class lecture can be written in note form this way:

> internatl studs rank adjust probs to Am study

Which words are abbreviated? Which words were left out?

Now using your own abbreviations and symbols, rewrite sentences one and four. Compare your notes with your classmates.

_____

_____

7. Making Notes: The Supporting Details

In the space below, take notes on the results of the survey as the teacher goes over the information. Practice using your note-taking abbreviations. **●-●**

1. _____   _____%
2. _____   _____%
3. _____   _____%
4. _____   _____%
5. _____   _____%
6. _____   _____%
7. _____   _____%
8. _____   _____%

After You Listen

8. Can You Find Out?

1. As the teacher pointed out, the survey applies to any kind of student. By yourself or in a group, make another survey directly related to international students on American campuses. Give your survey to as many students as possible. Report the results to your class.

2. Use the same items you heard on the tape and survey as many non-international students as possible. Change the words to "which did you expect to be." Put the results together and share the answers with your classmates.

3. Write a letter or make a cassette-tape letter to a friend back at home. Advise your friend about study in the United States. For example, "Before you come here you should know . . . ," "You should bring . . . ," "After you are here . . ."

4. Invite the international student advisor to talk to your class. Find out what on-campus and off-campus help is available to you.

5. Go to the library and look up the original research in the ERIC system (ERIC 224 419). What did the group of students expect to be the easiest adjustment?

9. Discussion

1. Why do students decide to study in the United States? What effect does American study have on students from your country, if any? Are there adjustment problems when students return to their own countries? What are they? Are they the same or different for men and women?

2. How did you choose your major field of study? Did your family help you make the choice? Will it be easy to find a job in your field? Would you consider working in another country? Why?

Jobs for Women and Men

OCCUPATION	#♂	%♂	#♀	%♀	TOTAL #♂♀
MGRS					5,232,023
PROD SUPERS					1,888,811
ASSMBLRS					1,700,083
COOKS					1,351,215
ELEM TCHRS					2,316,354

Before You Listen

1. What's Your Opinion?

Make a list of jobs in your home country which are mostly done by women. Make another list of jobs mostly done by men. Compare lists with your classmates. Do women and men generally have the same jobs or are the jobs different? Who is usually in a position of authority? Why?

2. Can You Predict?

Study the list of occupations in the chart. With a partner, decide what the occupations are. Which occupations have more authority? After you have discussed this, estimate what percentage of women are in each occupation.

As You Listen

3. Do You Know These Words?

Listen to some words and phrases taken from part of the class lecture. You will hear each word or phrase in a sentence. You will also hear the spelling. Write down the word or phrase on the lines below. After you finish, find the meanings in the right-hand column.

1. _____

2. _____

3. _____

4. _____

5. _____

6. _____

7. _____

a. after thinking about it, the only thing we can believe

b. but in contrast or while on the other hand

c. have jobs that allow control of a business or part of a business

d. held

e. in the lowest position

f. jobs in which people have the power to control and command others

g. number that shows some information

8. _____

9. _____

h. people in charge of, or
responsible for, workers and
the things the workers are
making

i. period of ten years

j. printed collection of numbers or information arranged
in rows across the page and
down the page

10. _____

11. _____

k. say that

12. _____

l. strongly controlled

13. _____

m. upsetting

n. workers who put together
something, such as a

14. _____

machine

Now listen for these words and phrases in the recording. ▪▪•

4. *Were You Right?*

Look at the chart again as you listen to the tape. Were your estimates about the percentage of women in each of the job categories relatively correct? ▪▪•

5. *Identify the Focus*

Three sentences below have similar meanings. Put a check mark (✓) next to them. What's different about the remaining sentence? Now listen for the words that focus attention on the main idea in this part of the class presentation. ▪▪•

1. The jobs having authority continue to be mostly held by men.

2. Males still work in the jobs with the most authority.

3. The occupational positions of authority continue to be dominated by males.

4. The occupational positions of authority will continue to be dominated by males.

Which words did you actually hear? Can you think of another sentence with the same meaning?

6. Making Notes: The Focus

The focus of the student's objection to the teacher's comment can be written in note form this way:

occupa'nl pos of auth — dom by ♂

Which words are abbreviated? Which words were left out? What symbols are used?

Now using your own abbreviations and symbols, rewrite sentences one and two. Compare your notes with your classmates.

_____

_____

7. Making Notes: The Supporting Details

The student uses an interesting strategy to emphasize her point. She uses the actual numbers for men in the various occupations and the percentages for women in the occupations. This has the effect of making the numbers of men sound large and the numbers of women sound small.

For practice, take down the actual numbers and percentages she mentions in her comment. ▣

Occupation	Number of Men	Percentage of Women
_____	_____	_____
_____	_____	_____
_____	_____	_____
_____	_____	_____
_____	_____	_____

After You Listen

8. Can You Find Out?

1. Use your school catalog for the following exercise. Count the number of men and women in each department. How many men are there? How many women? How many women are full professors? What percentage of the school administration are women, i.e., president, vice-presidents, deans? Does your "research" support the comments by the student in this lesson?

2. Get permission to observe a lecture/discussion class (at your school or another school). Observe the interaction of the class members and the instructor. Use a record sheet similar to the following example.

Male asks question   _____

Female asks question   _____

Male makes statement   _____

Female makes statement   _____

Teacher addresses male student   _____

Teacher addresses female student   _____

Did you observe any pattern in the class? What was it, if any?

3. Study the list of occupations below. Why did the newspaper publish the list? What was the Supreme Court decision? Does your country have any laws to balance the number of women/minorities in different occupations? Do these statistics agree with the student's comments? Explain your answer.

Working Women

Wednesday, the Supreme Court held that federal civil rights laws permit employers to take the sex of workers into account in hiring and promotion decisions to improve the representation of women in the workforce. Here's a sampling of occupations and the percentage of women holding them:

Occupation	*All Workers, Men, Women*	*Percent Women*
Architects	132,000	9.7%
Engineers	1,749,000	6%
Teachers (college)	639,000	56.2%
Teachers (others)	3,559,000	73.4%
Lawyers*	655,191	13.1%
Judges*		
State	12,093	7.2%
Federal	753	7.4%
State legislators*	7,461	14.8%
Airline pilots, navigators	79,000	1.5%
Auto mechanics	871,000	1%
Waiters, waitresses	1,403,000	85.1%
Police officers	666,000	10.9%
Firefighters	218,000	2.2%
Newspaper executive editors*	3,408	12.4%
Editors/reporters*	251,000	50.5%
Bank tellers	482,000	91.8%

Occupation	All Workers, Men, Women	Percent Women
School bus drivers	415,000	50.4%
Taxi drivers	187,000	12.5%
Clergy	285,000	7.2%
Executives	12,642,000	36.8%

*1985 figures. All others from 1986.

Sources: Bureau of Labor Statistics, American Bar Association, American Society of Newspaper Editors, Fund for Modern Courts

Source: *St. Petersburg Times*, March 26, 1987.

9. Discussion

1. Many societies have been traditionally dominated by males. Why do you think that has been the case? Do you think that is generally appropriate for modern-day societies? Why? Do you think that is appropriate for present-day society in your home country? Why?

2. Read the list of occupations in the newspaper column that was taken from the *St. Petersburg Times*. Are there any occupations on that list that you think are just for men or just for women? Why do you feel that way? Do your classmates agree or disagree with you? Why?

USA Today

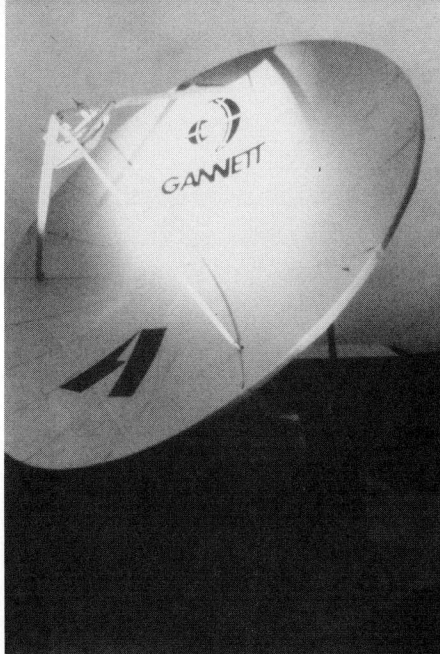

Before You Listen

1. What's Your Opinion?

How do you keep up with current events? Do you read a daily newspaper? listen to the radio? watch television? What's the difference between reading a newspaper and seeing the news on television? Which do you prefer? Why?

2. Can You Predict?

Until the appearance of *USA Today*, the U.S. had no daily national newspaper. Why do you think that was? What aspects of modern technology are necessary to publish and distribute a national newspaper?

As You Listen

3. Do You Know These Words?

Listen to some words and phrases taken from part of the class lecture. You will hear each word or phrase in a sentence. You will also hear the spelling. Write down the word or phrase on the lines below. After you finish, find the meanings in the right-hand column.

1. _____

2. _____

3. _____

4. _____

5. _____

6. _____

7. _____

a. a machine which moves through space high above the earth

b. machines that copy exactly whatever is on paper and change the copy to electronic impulses

c. machines that send narrow beams of light against something to "read" it

d. metal object that takes photographic images and is used for printing newspapers

e. object made of wires, metal rods, etc. which receives electronic impulses

f. places

g. powerful narrow line of light

8. _____ h. prepared for printing

9. _____ i. put together

10. _____ j. quickly looks at

11. _____ k. sent through space

l. the imaginary line around
the earth which is halfway
between its most northern

12. _____ and southern points

13. _____ m. treated

14. _____ n. uses light to produce

15. _____ o. very clear and easy to see

Now listen for these words and phrases in the recording. ▐●-●▌

4. Were You Right?

Look at the pictures again as you listen to the tape. Were your predictions about the technology of publishing a national newspaper right? ▐●-●▌

5. Identify the Focus

Three sentences below have similar meanings. Put a check mark (✔) next to them. What's different about the remaining sentence? Now listen for the words that focus attention on the main idea in this part of the class presentation. ▐●-●▌

1. It's modern technology that allows *USA Today* to publish a national newspaper.

2. *USA Today* can publish a nationwide daily paper because of modern technology.

3. Without this modern technology, it would be impossible for *USA Today* to publish a national daily newspaper.

4. With *USA Today's* modern technology, it's impossible to publish a national daily newspaper.

Which words did you actually hear? Can you think of another sentence with the same meaning?

6. Making Notes: The Focus

The focus of this description of the technology of publishing *USA Today* can be written in note form this way:

w/o mod tech — imposs to pub nat daily news

Which words are abbreviated? Which words were left out? What symbols are used?

Now using your own abbreviations and symbols, rewrite sentences one and two. Compare your notes with your classmates.

_____

_____

7. Making Notes: The Supporting Details

As you listen to the description, make notes below about the steps in the process of publishing the newspaper. ●-●

w/o mod tech — imposs to pub nat daily news

1. _____
2. _____
3. _____
4. _____
5. _____
6. _____
7. _____

After You Listen

8. Can You Find Out?

1. Arrange a tour of the local newspaper. How often is it published? What kind of technology is used?

2. Invite a student who works on the campus newspaper to the class. How often is it published? What kind of technology is available? How do they get news about the international student community?

3. Interview a number of people about *USA Today*. Find out if they read it and why or why not.

4. Find or draw a picture of a laser scanner, a facsimile machine, or a satellite. Explain how the one you chose operates.

5. Give a report on the most important (or most useless) development in modern technology. Use pictures, diagrams, charts, or any other visual material.

9. Discussion

1. Do you believe that the general public has a right to know everything that's going on in the world, or do you believe that there are some things that should be kept from the public? If you believe that some things should be kept from the public, what are some examples of those things? Who should decide which is which? Why?

2. We often hear that we are living in a "high-tech world." What does that phrase mean to you? Do you believe that the "high-tech" of today has a lot of influence on your day-to-day life? Why? In your own opinion, what are the good things and bad things that "high-tech" has brought into our lives? Why do you feel that way?

Adjusting to College Life

Before You Listen

1. What's Your Opinion?

What are the most common problems that university students in your home country have? How serious are those problems? If a student needs help in solving a problem, which people would that student be likely to go to? What help in problem solving would a college or university give a student in your home country?

2. Can You Predict?

In American universities, the international student advisor usually meets with new international students during the first week of the new term. The advisor gives information and advice about three general areas of student life. What do you think those three areas might be?

As You Listen

3. Do You Know These Words?

Listen to some words and phrases taken from part of the class lecture. You will hear each word or phrase in a sentence. You will also hear the spelling. Write down the word or phrase on the lines below. After you finish, find the meanings in the right-hand column.

1. _____   a. after a while or in the end

                               b. all the courses you wanted to
                                  enroll in were already filled
                                  with students and therefore
2. _____   closed

3. _____   c. at this school

4. _____   d. be solved

                               e. dormitory; building in which
5. _____   students live

6. _____   f. enrolled in or registered for

                               g. long, original compositions
                                  in which students combine
                                  information taken from
                                  different books, professional
                                  journals, etc., with their own
7. _____   ideas and conclusions

8. _____

9. _____

h. problems concerning a particular person that one may not
want others to know about

i. problems related to activities
with friends

j. problems related to changes
a person must make to be
able to live and work in a
new situation

10. _____

11. _____

k. problems related to study

l. tell you that you have
nothing to be afraid of

12. _____

13. _____

m. the official time students
enroll in classes

14. _____

n. too much to fight against

o. trying very, very hard or
fighting to solve the problems

15. _____

16. _____   p. very unhappy

Now listen for these words and phrases in the recording. ●-●

4. Were You Right?

As you listened to the student advisor, did you hear the three kinds
of problems all students might have? Was your prediction right about
the three? ●-●

5. Identify the Focus

Three sentences below have similar meanings. Put a check mark (✔)
next to them. What's different about the remaining sentence? Now
listen for the words that focus attention on the main idea in this part
of the class presentation. ●-●

1. All international students have some adjustment problems while
studying here.

2. All students from abroad report some problems adjusting while a
student here.

3. All students have some problems getting used to things as a
student here.

4. Problems of adjustment are part of student life for all foreign
students who study here.

Which words did you actually hear? Can you think of another sentence with the same meaning?

6. Making Notes: The Focus

The focus of these comments by the international student advisor can be written this way:

all internt'l studs → sm adjust probs study here

Which words are abbreviated? Which words were left out? What symbols are used?

Now using your own abbreviations and symbols, rewrite sentences two and four. Compare your notes with your classmates.

_____

_____

7. Making Notes: The Supporting Details

The advisor divided adjustment problems into three types and gave a few examples of each type. Use the outline below to take notes on the different problems. ●-●

1. _____

   e.g., _____

   _____

2. _____

   e.g., _____

   _____

3. _____

   e.g., _____

   _____

After You Listen

8. Can You Find Out?

1. Make a personal directory of campus people, organizations, and services. Where can you go for tutoring? Where can you go for information about classes and teachers? Where can you go for medical help? What other areas can you think of?

2. The movie *Ordinary People* was about communication problems in a middle-class American family. If you can, watch the movie and discuss it with your classmates. What do you think the problem was? How did the family solve it? How would you solve it?

3. Study the cartoon below. What is the problem? How did the professor solve the problem? What do you think of the solution? Would it be easy or difficult to talk to this teacher? Why?

"I'm afraid I've thoroughly messed up the seating chart, so you must take care to remember your new names."

Reprinted with permission. © 1984 Frank Cotham.

9. Discussion

1. Now and then problems arise in the daily lives of average people in every culture in the world. The types of problems might vary somewhat from culture to culture and so might ways of trying to deal with the problems. What are some common daily problems that average people have to deal with in your home country? How do people usually deal with those problems? How would you, yourself, deal with them?

   What seem to you to be some common daily problems that average Americans have? How do they seem to deal with those problems? How do you feel about that?

What kinds of problems have you had in the last few weeks? How have you tried to deal with them? What else could you have done?

2. Based on your own experience, what kind of relationship do teachers and students generally have in your home country? How about in the U.S.?

What's the best thing about relationships between teachers and students in your home country? What's the worst thing? How about in the U.S.?

Recycling Waste Water

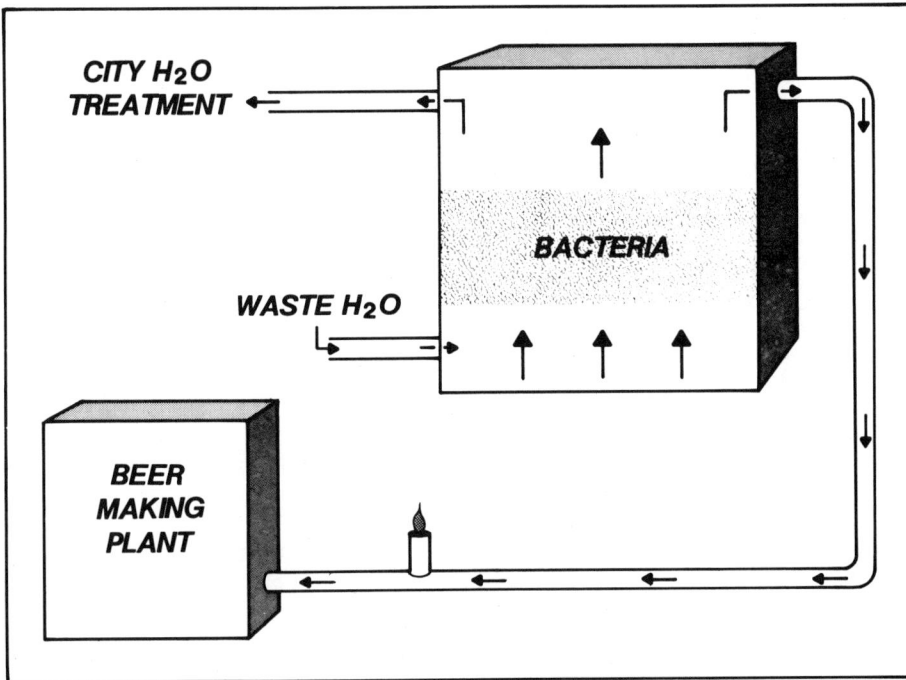

CITY H$_2$O
TREATMENT

BACTERIA

WASTE H$_2$O

BEER
MAKING
PLANT

Before You Listen

1. What's Your Opinion?

At your home do members of your family keep some things instead of throwing them away? For example, bags? newspapers? soda cans or bottles? How are those things used again? Do you think finding ways to use things again in a new way is a good idea? In your city, is there a program to recycle metals or paper? Why or why not?

2. Can You Predict?

Many industries use a lot of water, so it is important to recycle water. For example, when beer is made, waste water is left over. That waste water can be changed into something useful. What do you think it can be changed into? How can it be changed?

As You Listen

3. Do You Know These Words?

Listen to some words and phrases taken from part of the class lecture. You will hear each word or phrase in a sentence. You will also hear the spelling. Write down the word or phrase on the lines below. After you finish, find the meanings in the right-hand column.

1. _____

2. _____

3. _____

4. _____

5. _____

6. _____

7. _____

a. a continued set of actions that involve very, very small living things that live without air

b. air, water, land, and everything in nature that we see and feel around us

c. any unwanted thing that is leftover or unavoidably made while making something else

d. a way out for a liquid or a gas

e. chemicals or foods that provide for life and growth

f. covering

g. have as food

8. _____

9. _____

10. _____

11. _____

12. _____

13. _____

14. _____

15. _____

16. _____

17. _____

h. if not

i. is made cleaner and freer of harmful matter

j. make dirty

k. make something that has already been used, usable again

l. odorless, colorless gas (CH_4)

m. pass through and become clear

n. place where a city's waste water and waste material is chemically treated

o. plans

p. step-by-step making of things by factories and large organizations

q. very small living things that can only be seen through a microscope

Now listen for these words and phrases in the recording. [●-●]

4. Were You Right?

Look at the drawing again as you listen to the tape. Were your predictions about what waste water can be changed into correct? [●-●]

5. Identify the Focus

Three sentences below have similar meanings. Put a check mark (✔) next to them. What's different about the remaining sentence? Now listen for the words that focus attention on the main idea in the teacher's description of waste-water treatment. [●-●]

1. A bacteria process recovers beer and waste water from a treatment tank.

2. Recycling waste water through a bacteria process produces clear water and useful methane gas for the company.

3. The beer company that we're looking at changes waste water into methane gas and clear water.

4. Waste water recycled from beer production yields methane gas and clear water.

Which words did you actually hear? Can you think of another sentence with the same meaning?

6. Making Notes: The Focus

The focus of this description of recycling waste water can be written in note form this way:

beer co chgs waste $H_2O \rightarrow CH_4$ + clr H_2O

Which words are abbreviated? Which words were left out? What symbols are used?

Now using your own abbreviations and symbols, rewrite sentences two and four. Compare your notes with your classmates.

_____

_____

7. Making Notes: The Supporting Details

With a partner study the notes about the water recycling process below. Match the notes with the diagram. Then listen again to the description. Use your own abbreviations and symbols to take notes as you listen. |●-●|

bact eats nutrnts & mats in waste H_2O

$CH_4 \rightarrow$ beer co $\rightarrow$ use fr htg

clr $H_2O \rightarrow$ sewage treatment plant $\rightarrow$ re-use again

4/5 hrs fr H_2O ↑ thru bact

2 prods: clr H_2O + CH_4

waste $H_2O \rightarrow$ bottm tank

beer co chgs waste $H_2O \rightarrow CH_4$ + clr H_2O

1. _____

2. _____

3. _____

4. _____

5. _____

6. _____

After You Listen

8. Can You Find Out?

1. Read the news story below. What was the barge towing? Where did it try to deliver its cargo? What was the problem? What recycling need does this point to?

2. Some states have a law about recycling soft drink bottles and cans. Usually people strongly like or dislike this kind of law. Interview a number of people about why they like or dislike this idea. Then persuade your classmates to "vote" for or against the law.

3. Choose another example of recycling waste materials like the beer company example. Make a simple diagram of the process. Explain this process to your classmates.

4. Trash is one of the major exports for the United States. Go to the library and find out who exports and who imports this "product." What happens to the trash?

5. Yard sales (or garage sales) are very usual ways Americans recycle used, but usable, goods. Spend a Saturday or Sunday morning going to some sales in your area. You can find them in the classified ads in the newspaper. Take a tape recorder along and interview some of the buyers and sellers. Summarize your experience for your classmates.

9. Discussion

1. Is it really helpful for an average person to try to recycle household items? Who can that help? Does it help the individual who recycles the items? Does it help society?

   Is it really helpful for an average person to try to avoid polluting the environment? What are some common household items that might pollute the environment? (For example, laundry detergent or dishwashing liquid.) Are there nonpolluting substitutes available?

2. Should a national government set stadards to control pollution? Does your government? What programs do you know about? Are there programs like that that you support? How strict are the laws against pollution? How strict do you think they ought to be?

Smelly, Rotten, Stinking Garbage Could Become Valuable Export

New York Daily News

Can the rest of the world take America's garbage?

With U.S. dumps quickly reaching their capacities, waste management companies are trying to turn their smelly commodity into a profitable export, selling garbage to underdeveloped countries that need the money and landfilling.

Philadelphia expects to be the first city in the nation to set its ash —burned garbage—adrift. Starting in July, a contractor hired by the city will ship the ash down to Panama, said Pennsylvania Department of Environmental Resources spokesman William Apgar.

"It's cheaper to take it to Panama than Ohio," where many cities send ash, said Apgar. And the plan frees elected officials from dealing with public opposition to local landfills, he added.

A spokeswoman for the Panamanian consulate said the government has made no promises to take the ash. "The government is not interested," said Yolanda Alicia.

But the waste management industry is still promoting the idea. New York City was approached by several companies offering to take its garbage to the Caribbean, said Sanitation Department spokesman Vito Turso. But the city rejected the proposals because it seemed unlikely that other countries would want New York's garbage, he said.

The concept also is opposed by many waste experts and environmentalists as unfair and unworkable.

"I think it's totally immoral to take our waste piles and transport them to other countries that may not understand the environmental or health implications," said Walter Hang, a scientist with the New York Public Interest Research Group.

And Hugh Kaufman, a solid waste expert with the federal Environmental Protection Agency, said the idea is simply a way for the industry to avoid American regulations. "Waste material goes in the direction of least regulation and most lawlessness," he said.

No laws prohibit the export of municipal waste, which is controlled by the states. However, the federal government may intercede if the waste is deemed hazardous— often the case with garbage ash, Kaufman said.

However, the public's "fear of garbage" is likely to generate support for dumping it on a foreign country, said Donald Aulenbach, an environmental engineering professor at Rensselaer Polytechnic Institute. "Everyone wants to generate waste, but nobody wants to take responsibility for it," he said.

Wayward Barge Still Unwanted
Associated Press

NEW YORK—The hapless garbage barge, shunned by a half-dozen states and three countries, sat off the coast of Brooklyn on Sunday, its destination a matter of growing political and legal debate.

The barge of garbage steamed up the coast of New Jersey on Saturday and anchored at about 11 p.m. several hundred yards offshore in Gravesend Bay, about 700 yards south of the Verrazano-Narrows Bridge.

But the garbage's fate remained unclear. On Saturday, a judge issued an order temporarily barring the barge from docking in Queens.

Mayor Edward Koch said he did not oppose allowing the barge to dock in Queens, provided there are closed trucks on the site ready to immediately unload the garbage and take it to Islip, its original home.

The Bradenton Herald, May 18, 1987.

UNIT 20

The Scientific Method

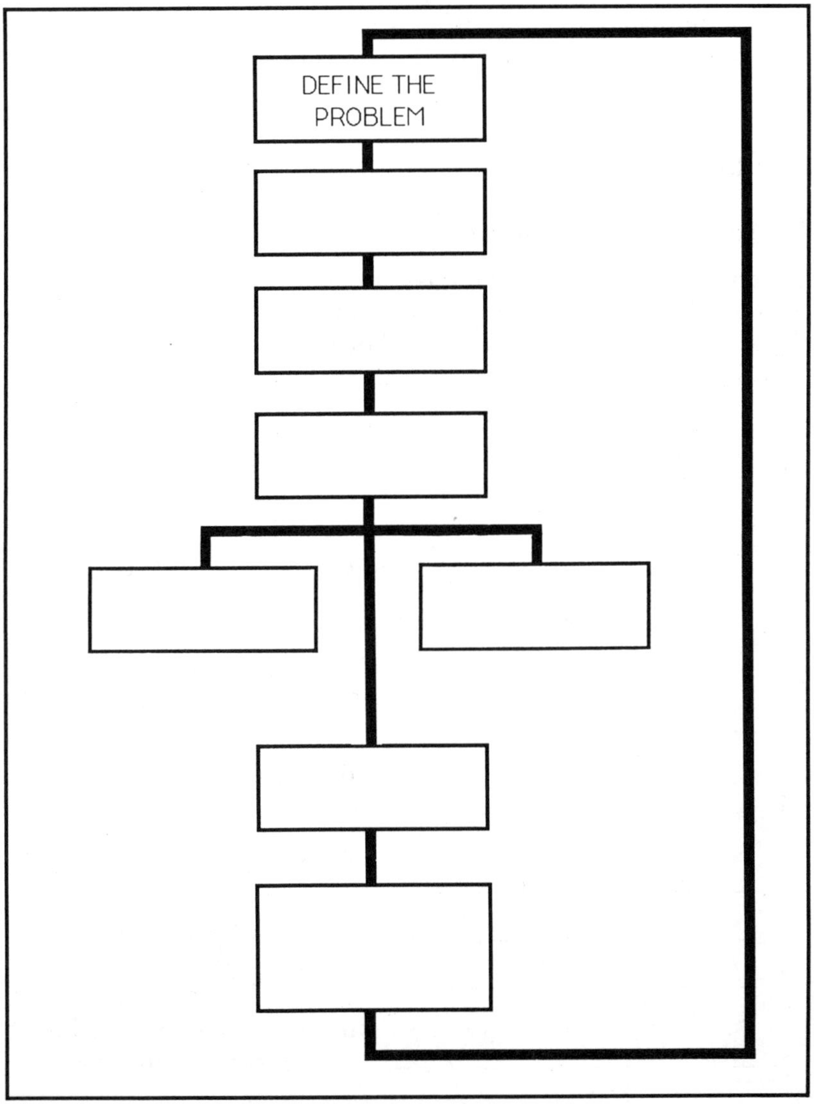
DEFINE THE PROBLEM

Adapted with permission of the publisher from *Sociology* by Richard T. Schaefer. © 1983 by McGraw-Hill Book Company.

Before You Listen

1. *What's Your Opinion?*

What was your favorite class in high school? Why did you like it? In general, do you like science courses or nonscience courses? How are science courses different from other classes? Do you think there is a "typical" science teacher or science student? Describe such a person.

2. *Can You Predict?*

The scientific method is a step-by-step way of problem-solving or learning new information. The first step is to define the problem. Do you remember what the other steps are? If not, can you and your classmates make reasonable guesses as to what they are?

As You Listen

3. *Do You Know These Words?*

Listen to some words and phrases taken from part of the class lecture. You will hear each word or phrase in a sentence. You will also hear the spelling. Write down the word or phrase on the lines below. After you finish, find the meanings in the right-hand column.

1. _____

2. _____

a. ask questions of many people to find out a general opinion

b. careful examination

c. carefully make up a clearly worded statement which seems suitable to explain something and which is used as a starting point for more study

3. _____

d. clearly show what a problem is

4. _____

e. clearly understand and becoming able to use

5. _____

6. _____

f. examine carefully

7. _____

g. facts or information

h. final opinion based on the known information

8. _____

9. _____   i.   give a question for everyone to consider

10. _____   j.   lead us to

                      k.   read what has been written

11. _____   on the subject in the past

12. _____   l.   separate

                    m.   study of a subject so as to

13. _____   learn new facts

                     n.   the actual study that we are

14. _____   to do in this class

15. _____   o.   understand

                     p.   written report on a detailed

16. _____   study of something

Now listen for these words and phrases in the recording.

4. Were You Right?

Look at the diagram again as you listen to the tape. Did you guess all of the steps? Did you get them in the right order?

5. Identify the Focus

Three sentences below have similar meanings. Put a check mark (✔) next to them. What's different about the remaining sentence? Now listen for the words that focus attention on the main idea in this part of the class presentation.

1. Five separate steps are followed when using the scientific method.

2. Scientists use five distinct methods in their experiments.

3. There are five distinct steps within the scientific method.

4. The scientific method consists of five different steps.

Which words did you actually hear? Can you think of another sentence with the same meaning?

6. Making Notes: The Focus

The focus of this part of the class lecture can be written in note form this way:

scientific meth → 5 steps

Which words are abbreviated? Which words were left out? What symbols are used?

Now using your own abbreviations and symbols, rewrite sentences one and four. Compare your notes with your classmates.

_____

_____

7. Making Notes: The Supporting Details

Use the outline here to take notes on the steps in the scientific method. $\boxed{\bullet\text{-}\bullet}$

scientfc meth → 5 steps

1. def prob

2. _____

3. _____

4. _____

    a. _____

    b. _____

5. _____

After You Listen

8. Can You Find Out?

1. Invite a teacher from the philosophy department to talk to your class about Aristotle. What is the relationship of this Greek philosopher to the scientific method?

2. Observe a beginning chemistry or physics class conducting an experiment. Take notes on each step in the experiment. Report on your observations to your classmates.

3. Imagine that you are a famous scientist. You have made a very important discovery that will change everyone's life. What is it? How did you find it?

4. Give a report on a famous scientific experiment in history. If you can, show the class the experiment. Why did you choose this experiment?

5. Formulate a hypothesis about the students on your campus. Conduct a survey to collect some information. Analyze the data and report the results to your class.

9. Discussion

1. What do you think is the most important scientific advance of this century? Why? What about the future? In your opinion, what is the most exciting scientific event you can imagine?

2. Do you think the scientific method is useful in everyday life? How do/can you use it? Would a careful methodical approach to problem-solving be useful to you?

PART TWO

UNIT 21

Persuasion in Speaking

Before You Listen

1. What's Your Opinion?

Are there any speakers whom you especially like to listen to? Who are they? What kinds of things make you interested in hearing someone speak?

2. Can You Predict?

Look at the illustrations showing three different people in speaking situations. What seems to be wrong in each picture? What is the reason it is wrong?

As You Listen

3. Do You Know These Words?

Listen to some words and phrases taken from part of the class lecture. You will hear each word or phrase in a sentence. You will also hear the spelling. Write down the word or phrase on the lines below. After you finish, find the meanings in the right-hand column.

1. _____ a. co-worker

2. _____ b. defect

3. _____ c. done smoothly

4. _____ d. examination to learn about

5. _____ e. horrible

6. _____ f. make up

7. _____ g. not deep

8. _____ h. not likely to be wrong

9. _____ i. part

10. _____ j. put together

11. _____ k. racial background

12. _____ l. situation

                                   m. that part completing and
13. _____   adding to the whole

14. _____ n. very important

Now listen for these words and phrases in the recording. ▮●-●▮

4. Were You Right?

Look at the pictures again as you listen to the tape. Which speaker is *not* appealing to emotions? To reason? To credibility? ▮●-●▮

5. Identify the Focus

Three sentences below have similar meanings. Put a check mark (✔) next to them. What's different about the remaining sentence? Now listen for the words that focus attention on the main idea in this part of the class presentation. ▮●-●▮

1. Aristotle enumerated three kinds of persuasion.

2. Aristotle says there are basically three types of persuasion.

3. There are three different ways to convince someone of something, according to Aristotle.

4. There are three types of speeches, according to Aristotle.

6. Making Notes: The Focus

The focus of this part of the class lecture can be written in note form this way:

Arist → 3 kinds per

Which words are abbreviated? Which words were left out? What symbols are used?

Now using your own abbreviations and symbols, rewrite sentences one and three.

_____

_____

7. Making Notes: The Supporting Details

Below are Aristotle's three types of persuasion. Define each one. Give examples for each one. ▮●-●▮

1. Ethos — defined as: _____

   e.g., _____

   _____

2. Pathos — defined as: _____

   e.g., _____

   _____

3. Logos — defined as: _____

   e.g., _____

   _____

After You Listen

8. Can You Find Out?

1. Is public speaking taught in your home country? In high school? At the university level? At a special kind of school? If public speaking is taught there, who are the people who take it? What is their purpose in taking it?

2. Interview a speech teacher. Find out how important that teacher feels an accent is and the reasons why the teacher feels that way.

3. In the past, U.S. President Ronald Reagan was often called "The Great Communicator." Try to interview one or more speech teachers and one or more political science teachers or a local politician and find out what their opinions are as to why Mr. Reagan was called that. Are their opinions similar or different?

4. Find out which students in your class regularly watch the evening news on TV. Find out which anchor person has the highest degree of credibility and why.

9. Discussion

1. Why do some people seem to you to have a higher degree of credibility than others? What qualities does a person need to gain your respect and trust? Is it mostly looks? Mostly actions? Both? Neither? Do you feel that you, yourself, have those qualities?

2. Have you ever gotten nervous because of having to talk in front of a group of people? What was the situation? What happened? What can people do to help prevent themselves from getting nervous in that situation?

3. Try to think of a person in your own country who is considered to be a good public speaker. Why do people think that? If that person could give speeches in the U.S., do you think that he or she would be considered good? Why?

The Basic Accounting Formula

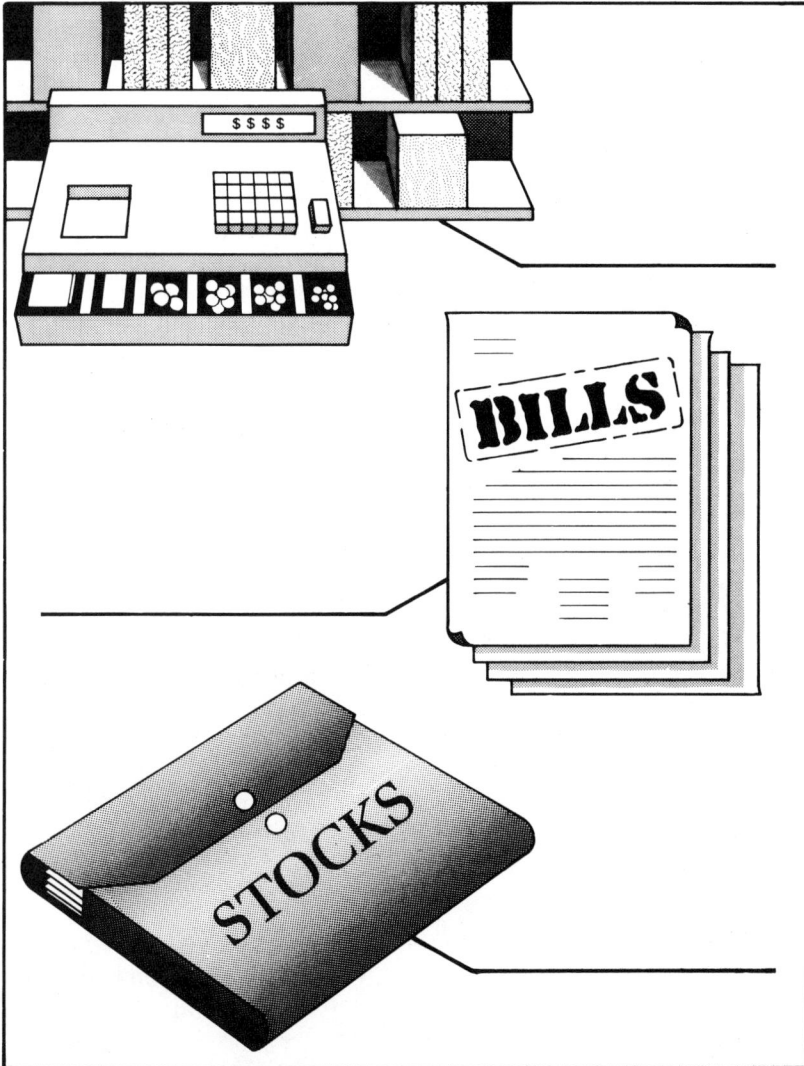

Before You Listen

1. What's Your Opinion?

What does accounting mean to you? How would you explain it to someone who does not know what it means? Why is accounting so important in business?

2. Can You Predict?

Look at the illustrations. Can you guess which drawing shows *assets?* Which one shows *liabilities?* How about *equity?*

As You Listen

3. Do You Know These Words?

Listen to some words and phrases taken from part of the class lecture. You will hear each word or phrase in a sentence. You will also hear the spelling. Write down the word or phrase on the lines below. After you finish, find the meanings in the right-hand column.

1. _____

2. _____

3. _____

4. _____

5. _____

6. _____

7. _____

8. _____

9. _____

10. _____

a. a board balanced in the middle

b. amount of money put into a business to make more money

c. a less simple word meaning things we owe

d. an indirect suggestion

e. anything used which helps in doing your job

f. are likely to

g. a simple word meaning things we owe

h. comparison

i. coming from

j. people who keep and examine business accounts

11. _____

12. _____

13. _____

14. _____

15. _____

k. staying informed about

l. things used in a store like the shelving or display cases

m. things we own

n. things we own minus things we owe

o. things we sell

Now listen for these words and phrases in the recording. 🔲

4. Were You Right?

Look at the illustrations again as you listen to the tape. Were your predictions about the pictures correct? 🔲

5. Identify the Focus

Three sentences below have similar meanings. Put a check mark (✔) next to them. What's different about the remaining sentence? Now listen for the words that focus attention on the main idea in this part of the class presentation. 🔲

1. The accounting formula which is fundamental is that one's assets are equal to one's liabilities and equity.

2. The basic accounting formula can be stated in the following: liabilities equal assets plus equity.

3. The fundamental accounting formula is that all we own is equal to a combination of our debts and investments.

4. Your basic accounting equation: assets equal liabilities plus equity.

Which words did you actually hear? Can you think of another sentence with the same meaning?

6. Making Notes: The Focus

The focus of this part of the class lecture can be written in note form this way:

$$A = L + E$$

Which words are abbreviated? Which words were left out? What symbols are used?

Now using your own abbreviations and symbols, rewrite sentences one and three. Compare your notes with your classmates.

_____

_____

7. Making Notes: The Supporting Details

On the lines below note down the examples given in the lecture to illustrate and explain each term. ▣▸▸●

Assets: _____

_____

Liabilities: _____

_____

Equity: _____

_____

After You Listen

8. Can You Find Out?

1. Is accounting taught in your home country? In high school? At the university level? At a special kind of school? If accounting is taught there, who are the people who take it? Is the idea of "accounting" pretty much the same in your home country as it is in the U.S. or is it different?

2. What percentage of students in your present school are business majors? Try to find out for both undergraduate and graduate level programs. Is this percentage higher or lower than last year? Can you find a trend in the number of students studying business? Is this similar to the situation in your home country?

3. What percentage of new, small businesses in the city you presently live in become bankrupt or go out of business every year? Is this higher or lower than in recent past years? What are some of the reasons for this?

9. Discussion

1. Are you interested in studying business? What do you like and dislike about business? Is business a popular major at universities

in your home country? Do you think everyone should have some degree of education in business? Why?

2. Do you think a liberal arts education is important and useful to a person who is a business major? Why?

3. Think of one or two stores in which you often shop. What is it about those stores that causes you to go back again and again? Think of one or two stores that you have been in, but don't like. What is it about those stores that causes you to dislike them?

4. In your honest opinion, do you think modern societies stress business and earning money too much? Why?

Nutrition

Before You Listen

1. What's Your Opinion?

Is there a relationship between good health and certain kinds of food? What food is healthy food? Is it possible to have unhealthy food? Why? Is eating an important activity for you or just something you do?

2. Can You Predict?

Protein is a nutrient found in meat, fish, and pork. What other nutrients do you know? What kinds of food are those nutrients found in?

As You Listen

3. Do You Know These Words?

Listen to some words and phrases taken from part of the class lecture. You will hear each word or phrase in a sentence. You will also hear the spelling. Write down the word or phrase on the lines below. After you finish, find the meanings in the right-hand column.

1. _____   a.   ability to be active

2. _____   b.   a disease causing a loss of
                                   calcium from the bones

3. _____   c.   a disease causing bones to
                                   soften

4. _____   d.   be dishonest

5. _____   e.   cavities, decay

                             f.   chemicals or food needed for
6. _____   life and growth

7. _____   g.   chickens, ducks, etc.

                             h.   consisting of many closely
8. _____   connected parts

9. _____   i.   greatly dislike

10. _____   j.   less than what is needed

                             k.   measure used for how much
                                  heat or energy a food will
11. _____   produce

12. _____ l. purpose

13. _____ m. reach

14. _____ n. too much

15. _____ o. very strong

Now listen for these words and phrases in the recording. [●••●]

4. *Were You Right?*

Look at the illustration again as you listen to the tape. Were your predictions about nutrients and kinds of food correct? [●••●]

5. *Identify the Focus*

Three sentences below have similar meanings. Put a check mark (✔) next to them. What's different about the remaining sentence? Now listen for the words that focus attention on the main idea in this part of the class presentation. [●••●]

1. There are six various kinds of nutrients that are spoken about in the course of a year.

2. The six different food groups are discussed during the year.

3. What we talk about all during the year are six different ways to eat.

4. What we talk about all during the year are the six classes of nutrients.

Which words did you actually hear? Can you think of another sentence with the same meaning?

6. *Making Notes: The Focus*

The focus of this part of the class lecture can be written in note form this way:

Nut → 6 class

Which words are abbreviated? Which words were left out? What symbols are used?

Now using your own abbreviations and symbols, rewrite sentences one and two. Compare your notes with your classmates.

_____

_____

7. Making Notes: The Supporting Details

On the lines below, note down the six classes of nutrients and give examples for each. Also list why each nutrient is important. ●-●

1. _____

   e.g., _____

   Reason important: _____

2. _____

   e.g., _____

   Reason important: _____

3. _____

   e.g., _____

   Reason important: _____

4. _____

   e.g., _____

   Reason important: _____

5. _____

6. _____

After You Listen

8. Can You Find Out?

1. Are there currently nutritional problems in your home country? Have there been serious nutritional problems in the past? When? How did people cope with the problem?

2. What is the major source of protein in the diet of an average person in your home country? How about the major source of carbohydrates? How does that differ from an average person's diet in the U.S.?

3. There are many one-a-day vitamins and minerals on the market. Go to a store, look over the vitamins and minerals, check the prices, and decide which ones seem to be best. Report back to the class.

4. For losing weight, there are many diet plans and aids for dieting on the market. Go to a store, look over them, and decide which

ones seem best and safest to you. Also choose one that looks like it might be a fake. Report back to the class.

9. *Discussion*

1. Do you make an effort to eat a balanced diet? What, in your diet, do you try to be careful with? Why? Do you take vitamins? Why?

2. Because of the extra work required of the heart, being overweight can be dangerous. Do you think there are more or less overweight people in your home country as there are in the U.S.? Why do you think that is? Have you, yourself, ever tried to lose weight? What did you do? Was it successful?

3. The number of people who are now interested in having a healthy lifestyle seems to continue to go up in the U.S. What changes do you think that interest has caused people to make in their lives? Are you, yourself, interested in having a healthy lifestyle? Why? How about people in your home country?

The Law of Demand

Before You Listen

1. What's Your Opinion?

How do prices of merchandise in the United States compare with those in your country? In general, have prices increased, decreased, or remained unchanged in the last year in the U.S.? Give examples.

2. Can You Predict?

Can you think of various reasons why people buy things? What is the most important reason?

As You Listen

3. Do You Know These Words?

Listen to some words and phrases taken from part of the class lecture. You will hear each word or phrase in a sentence. You will also hear the spelling. Write down the word or phrase on the lines below. After you finish, find the meanings in the right-hand column.

1. _____   a. buying habits

2. _____   b. cause

3. _____   c. decides

4. _____   d. fact helping to bring about a result

5. _____   e. given a reason for doing something

6. _____   f. have enough money to pay for

7. _____   g. important things

8. _____   h. is present

9. _____   i. place for selling old or used things

10. _____   j. separate

11. _____   k. something which changes

12. _____   l. very important

Now listen for these words and phrases in the recording. `[■•●]`

4. Were You Right?

Listen to the tape again. Were your predictions about why people buy things correct? ▣

5. Identify the Focus

Three sentences below have similar meanings. Put a check mark (✔) next to them. What's different about the remaining sentence? Now listen for the words that focus attention on the main idea in this part of the class presentation. ▣

1. What are the forces that motivate you to use credit cards for something?

2. What are the influences which cause you to buy something?

3. What motivates you to buy something?

4. What reasons do you have for purchasing something?

Which words did you actually hear? Can you think of another sentence with the same meaning?

6. Making Notes: The Focus

The focus of this part of the class lecture can be written in note form this way:

What motiv buy X

Which words are abbreviated? Which words were left out? What symbols are used?

Now using your own abbreviations and symbols, rewrite sentences two and four. Compare your notes with your classmates.

_____

_____

7. Making Notes: The Supporting Details

On the lines below note down the forces that influence the buying of something. Put a star next to the most important factor. ▣

_____

_____

_____

_____

After You Listen

8. Can You Find Out?

1. Interview a merchant and ask if he or she has actually seen proof of the law of demand as discussed in the lecture. If yes, find out the details of the situation and report back to the class.

2. Observe a commodity over a period of time and see what happens to its price. Try to come up with reasons for the changes in the price.

3. Interview a supermarket manager and find out how prices are set for items in the store. Also find out how they go about lowering or raising the prices of an item.

4. Is the economy of your home country closely linked to the U.S. economy? Why is that? How long has that situation existed? When did it start?

9. Discussion

1. When you do shopping and your choice of commodities is mainly based on the price, what kind of things are you buying? Are there some commodities that you usually buy regardless of the price? If so, what are they?

2. Is the basic economy of your home country based on capitalism? Is it based on communism? Can you think of both strong and weak points in each system? What are they? In recent years some communist governments have allowed some degree of capitalism to be practiced. Do you think this is a good idea or not? Why?

3. Do you feel the U.S. economy is currently stable? How about in your home country? What are you basing your feelings on? What kinds of things do you think generally signal a stable or unstable economy?

UNIT 25

The Judicial System

Before You Listen

1. What's Your Opinion?

Are there any crimes in your country that are considered serious but not in the U.S.? What crimes do you think are serious? What sorts of punishment should be given for them?

2. Can You Predict?

After someone has been arrested for a serious crime, various procedures in the judicial system are followed before that person is given punishment. Can you think of some of them?

As You Listen

3. Do You Know These Words?

Listen to some words and phrases taken from part of the class lecture. You will hear each word or phrase in a sentence. You will also hear the spelling. Write down the word or phrase on the lines below. After you finish, find the meanings in the right-hand column.

1. _____	a. break
2. _____	b. coming before
3. _____	c. declare oneself to be
4. _____	d. enough
5. _____	e. give the punishment
6. _____	f. judgement
7. _____	g. person who has broken the law
8. _____	h. prison
9. _____	i. starting a fire
10. _____	j. stealing money

Now listen for these words and phrases in the recording. [●–●]

4. Were You Right?

Were some of your predictions about procedures followed in the judicial system correct? [●–●]

5. Identify the Focus

Three sentences below have similar meanings. Put a check mark (✔) next to them. What's different about the remaining sentence? Now listen for the words that focus attention on the main idea in this part of the class presentation. ▣▪●▣

1. What are the procedures for dealing with an individual who has committed a serious crime?

2. What happens to a person when they are arrested for a felony offense?

3. What occurs when somebody is arrested for committing a misdemeanor?

4. When someone has broken an important law, how does the judicial system handle that person?

Which words did you actually hear? Can you think of another sentence with the same meaning?

6. Making Notes: The Focus

The focus of this part of the class lecture can be written in note form this way:

What hap per when arrest fel off

Which words are abbreviated? Which words were left out?
   Now using your own abbreviations and symbols, rewrite sentences one and four. Compare your notes with your classmates.

_____

_____

7. Making Notes: The Supporting Details

On the lines below trace the path a person follows in the judicial system after being arrested for a felony offense. ▣▪●▣

Person   →   →   →
Arrested   _____   _____

_____   →   _____   → Penitentiary

After You Listen

8. Can You Find Out?

1. What happens to a person in your home country from the time of his arrest to the time of his sentencing? In what aspects is it similar to the U.S. system? In what aspects is it different?

2. Laws and punishments vary a lot from country to country. What is typical and common in one country may seem harsh and extreme in another. Go to a video shop and rent the movie *Midnight Express*. After watching the film, decide whether you think the punishment for the crime in that film was appropriate or inappropriate and discuss reasons why.

3. Interview someone whose work is related to the law, that is, a police officer, a lawyer, a judge, or someone like that, and find out what that person thinks the current most serious crimes are and what should be done about them. Report to the class.

4. Which developed countries allow capital punishment and which ones don't? What reasons do those countries give to explain why they do what they do?

9. Discussion

1. In general, how do you feel about the system of laws and the court system in your home country? Is it fair? Are most people treated the same? Why do you feel that way?

2. What are some of the things that are related to U.S. laws and the U.S. court system that surprised you when you first learned of them? Why were you surprised?

3. What experiences with police officers, the law, etc., have you, yourself, had in your home country or in the U.S.? Discuss the situation and how you felt at the time.

4. Why do you think some developed countries have a much higher crime rate than others? Do you think there is more or less crime in your home country as compared to the U.S.? Why do you think that is?

TAPESCRIPTS

Tapescript/Unit 1

Math Graduates

3. Do you know these words?
   1. *Anxious.*   I know that you're anxious to get into this course. *Anxious.*
   2. *Majors.*   Many of you are mathematics majors. *Majors.*
   3. *Statistical.*   Some math majors go directly into statistical jobs. *Statistical.*
   4. *Blue collar jobs.*   Some math majors take on blue collar jobs. *Blue collar jobs.*
   5. *Clerical.*   Some math majors end up in clerical jobs. *Clerical.*

I know that you're *anxious* to get in . . . to this course and begin work on the mathematical ideas and processes that the course will cover. I s . . . also see from your roll, the roll list that many of you are mathematics *majors*, and I think it might be good at the beginning of this course to say a few words about mathematics majors and the jobs that they end up doing to put the course into some perspective.

I think you should realize that **just because math is your major you're not going to end up in math-related jobs**. Not necessarily so. We have studies that show that yes, 13% of math majors do go directly into mathematics or *statistical* jobs. But there are other groups that don't go directly into math-related professions. For example, 12% of math majors end up in elementary or secondary teaching jobs; 4% become college teachers; 7% take on *blue collar jobs*, another 7% become managers; 16% of math majors end up in *clerical* jobs. Another 4% in service jobs, 1% in retail sales, 7% in other occupations. There is a large group, 30% who end up as, uh, computer specialists, so there's a field related to mathematics. In fact, 59% end up in math-related professions, but another 41% end up in other nonmathematical professions.

Tapescript/Unit 2

The Hydrologic Process

3. Do you know these words?
   1. *The hydrologic process.*   The hydrologic process is a process of evaporation and precipitation. *The hydrologic process.*

2. *Evaporation.*   Evaporation and precipitation, did you get that? *Evaporation.*

3. *Precipitation.*   Now precipitation is either rain or snow or hail. *Precipitation.*

4. *Aquifers.*   It might go into aquifers, which are rocks that hold water. *Aquifers.*

5. *Transpiration.*   This evaporation is called transpiration. *Transpiration.*

6. *Atmosphere.*   It will go into the atmosphere as a kind of water vapor. *Atmosphere.*

7. *Water vapor.*   When this water vapor cools off, it will become clouds. *Water vapor.*

OK, if you'll, uh, just focus your attention on the screen, we'll discuss *the hydrologic process* now. And the hydrologic process is a cycle like others that we've seen throughout this semester. Uh, basically what it is, **the hydrologic process is a process of *evaporation* and *precipitation.*** Evaporation and precipitation, did you get that? OK and you start with pre-cipitation. Now precipitation, what that is, is either rain or snow or hail, in other words, water, that falls to the earth. And it may fall to a variety of locations on the earth. Uh, if it goes to the soil, soil, it may go to under-ground water sources or it might go into *aquifers*, which are rocks that hold water. Uh, if it doesn't go into the soil, it might just be evaporated, uh, when the sun comes out with the heat and this evaporation, is called *transpiration.* Uh, if the, the precipitation falls to the lakes and rivers, eventually it'll probably end up in the ocean and it will evaporate there and uh, it will go into the *atmosphere* as a kind of *water vapor.* Uh, when the, uh, when when this water vapor cools off, it will become clouds, and if the wind comes and pushes it around awhile eventually the whole process starts over again with rain and snow and hail. So we really do have a, a continuous process here.

Tapescript/Unit 3

Life Expectancy

3. Do you know these words?

1. *Life expectancy.*   Life expectancy is not the same all around the world. *Life expectancy.*

2. *Column.*   Take a look at the very last column. *Column.*

3. *Poorest countries.*   In the poorest countries, people don't live very long. *Poorest countries.*

4. *The entire range.* Let's take a look at the entire range of life expectancies. *The entire range.*

5. *Categories.* There are five categories of life expectancies. *Categories.*

6. *The most developed countries.* People live longest in the most developed countries. *The most developed countries.*

All right class, today let's take a look at *life expectancy* around the world. If you take a look here at the map and the chart up on the screen, you can see that **life expectancy is not the same all around the world**. For example, take a look at the very last *column*. In the *poorest countries*, people don't even live to be 39. Let's take a look at, uh, *the entire range* or the five *categories* of life expectancies. As we can see in *the most developed countries*, in North America, Australia, USSR, Japan, and Europe, people live to be 70 or more. In the next category, most of South America, China, Philippines, and Hong Kong, the expectancy is between 60 and 69. In the third category—most of the Middle East and many Southeast Asian countries—the expectancy is 50 to 59 years of age. In the fourth category, Central and South Africa, people live to be 40 to 49 years of age. And as I stated earlier, in some of the very poorest countries, if you take a look here on the map, Afghanistan, Bolivia, Laos, and Mali, people live to be 39 years or less.

Tapescript/Unit 4

World Energy Sources

3. Do you know these words?

1. *Accounts for.* Oil accounts for much of our energy supply. *Accounts for.*

2. *Energy supply.* Oil accounts for much of our energy supply. *Energy supply.*

3. *Fossil fuels.* Oil, coal, and gas are all fossil fuels. *Fossil fuels.*

4. *Energy source.* A lot of our energy source comes from fossil fuels. *Energy source.*

5. *Garbage and refuse.* Some of our energy comes from garbage and refuse. *Garbage and refuse.*

6. *At the very bottom.* At the very bottom we have water. *At the very bottom.*

7. *That's really it.* That's really it for our energy sources. *That's really it.*

Let's turn now to energy sources. Uh, did you hear that? Energy sources. Leaving out solar energy, **what you have in the world is** basically **five different sorts of energy**. Uh, the first and the largest is oil, this *accounts for* about 36% of our *energy supply*. Next we have coal at 28%. And, uh, another one, of course, is, is natural gas, that's about 17%. And these three different kinds of energy are all *fossil fuels*, and they account for a total of about 80%. So that's really quite a lot of our *energy source* coming from fossil fuels. Uh, next we have, of course, wood and *garbage and refuse* and other, other energy sources such as that, that accounts for about 19%. And *at the very bottom* we have water or hydropower, which is about 1% of our world energy sources, uh, and *that's really it* for our energy sources.

Tapescript/Unit 5

Population Movements

3. Do you know these words?
   1. *Social changes.*   There have been many social changes in American life over the past few years. *Social changes.*
   2. *Shifts.*   Shifts have occurred in the American population. *Shifts.*
   3. *Sunbelt.*   We've heard a lot about the general move from the colder sections of the country to the sunbelt. *Sunbelt.*
   4. *Rural areas.*   Rural areas, in the United States, surpassed urban areas. *Rural areas.*
   5. *Surpassed.*   Rural areas surpassed urban areas. *Surpassed.*
   6. *Urban areas.*   Rural areas surpassed urban areas. *Urban areas.*
   7. *In terms of.*   Rural areas, in the United States, surpassed urban areas in terms of the rate of population growth. *In terms of.*
   8. *Dramatic.*   The shift is even more dramatic in the western section of the country. *Dramatic.*
   9. *Overall.*   Overall, we see that these areas grew faster than those. *Overall.*

Any course concerned with important *social changes* in American life over the past few years must look at the growth in population in the United States and *shifts* that have, have occurred in the, uh, American population.

We've heard a lot about the general move from the older, colder sections of the country to the *sunbelt*, to the south and the western areas. But within the regions, we see some interesting movement of population when we compare the growth of the cities and the, the country areas.

From 1970 to 1980 *rural areas* in the United States *surpassed urban areas in terms of* the rate of population growth. For example, in the northeast section the city areas lost 1.8% of their populations but the rural areas gained 12.8%. So, too, in the north-central area, the cities lost 2.2% but the countryside gained 8%. The shift is even more *dramatic* in the western section of the country, where cities grew 21.9% but the rural areas grew even more, 32.2%. It's only in the, the southern states where we have, uh, the cities, uh, growing faster than the rural areas. The cities grew in the south at 21.2% and the rural areas grew at 17.8%. But *overall* when we look at all of the regions together, we see that in the 1970s to 1980 period, uh, the rural areas grew faster than the urban areas.

Tapescript/Unit 6

A Child's Motor Skills

3. Do you know these words?
   1. *Pattern.*   There is a definite pattern of development. *Pattern.*
   2. *Prenatal.*   There is a definite pattern in prenatal human development. *Prenatal.*
   3. *Stage.*   There is a definite pattern of development in the prenatal stage of human development. *Stage.*
   4. *Motor skills development.*   Motor skills development follows a certain order. *Motor skills development.*
   5. *Motor skills.*   A child's motor skills are usually developed in a certain sequence. *Motor skills.*
   6. *Sequence.*   A child's motor skills are usually developed in a certain sequence. *Sequence.*
   7. *Exact.*   These months are not exact times. *Exact.*
   8. *Specific.*   These months are not exact times when a child will learn this specific skill. *Specific.*

   Yes, you're right. Just as we saw that there is a definite *pattern* of development in the *prenatal stage* of human development, remember now that . . . that pattern doesn't stop at birth. In fact, it continues well into the first years of life. OK, let's take for example *motor skills development.* Now, **a child's *motor skills* are usually developed in a certain *sequence.*** Now according to the chart in front of you, OK, there's certain months listed. OK, from one month to fifteen months, and then it shows, uh, the different skills that the child learns. Now for any of you who are parents in the class, you'll know that this is, uh, the months here are not *exact* times when a child will learn this *specific* skill. But what's important from this chart is that one skill is learned before the next one is. OK? So let's take for example one month. At one month a child, uh, learns how to hold its chin up while learning, lying on its stomach. Then at three months, OK, after the child learns how to keep its chin up, the child begins to reach out for things. That's when it's time to clear the coffee table. After that, a few months after that, on or about six months, the child begins to hold on to things. And then at seven months, again the child learns to sit alone. And after that, at around somewhere around eleven months—now remember these are not exact . . . times for a child learning this skill—but somewhere around eleven months a child learns to walk with help. Uh, then after that, the child learns how to climb. OK, that's when you start seeing the bumps and the black and blue marks on the baby. OK, and then at around fifteen months a child learns how to walk alone and, uh, that's a . . . a big time for parents. Now of course, uh, none of this again is new information for those of you who are parents in the class.

Tapescript/Unit 7

Completing High School

3. Do you know these words?
   1. *Assume.*   It's safe to assume that most of you have graduated from high school. *Assume.*
   2. *Natural.*   Assuming that everyone has graduated from high school seems natural these days. *Natural.*
   3. *Majority.*   A majority of people in the United States complete high school. *Majority.*
   4. *Complete.*   A majority of people in the United States complete high school. *Complete.*
   5. *That has not always been the case.*   Many graduate now, but that has not always been the case. *That has not always been the case.*
   6. *Rose.*   Later that percentage rose slightly. *Rose.*
   7. *Slightly.*   Later that percentage rose slightly. *Slightly.*
   8. *Figures.*   These figures show the percentage of adults who have completed high school. *Figures.*

Since you're sitting in a college classroom, it's probably safe to *assume* that most of you've graduated from high school. That seems *natural* these days, and it's true that a *majority* of people in the United

States, uh, do *complete* high school. But *that has not always been the case.* If we look back 30 years, say to, to 1950, we see that only 38% of adults in the United States graduated from high school. Ten years later in 1960 that percentage *rose slightly* to 42%, and by 1970 the percentage has, had risen to 60%. By 1975, 69% of adults in the United States had completed high school, and in 1981 we have the highest percentage so far, 77% of, uh, adults in the United States have completed high school. So when we, when we look back over those *figures* we see that **the percentage of adults who have completed high school in this country has increased since 1950.**

Tapescript/Unit 8

Large Families

3. Do you know these words?
    1. *Fluctuation.* There's been a general fluctuation of attitude towards large families. *Fluctuation.*
    2. *Attitude.* There's been a general fluctuation of attitude towards large families. *Attitude.*
    3. *Favored.* The number of people who have favored large families was up ten years later. *Favored.*
    4. *Decline.* After the rise, there was a decline. *Decline.*
    5. *Sharp.* The decline was very sharp. *Sharp.*
    6. *Slight.* After the decline there was a slight rise up. *Slight.*
    7. *Factors.* Many factors affect people's attitudes towards large families. *Factors.*
    8. *Affect.* Many factors affect people's attitudes towards large families. *Affect.*

In some parts of the world, having a large family can be a sign of power and prestige. And, uh, in the United States at some points throughout our history, that was also true. As a matter of fact, I am from a very large family myself; I have eleven brothers and sisters. Yes, it's very unusual isn't it? Uh, at one time, again, this was a very popular thing, to have a large family. But uh, it hasn't always been that way. Uh, in fact, **there's been a general *fluctuation* of *attitude*, uh, towards large families in the United States.**

Let's go back, well first of all, let's look at this, uh, chart in front of us. Notice that in, in the year 1936, OK, 34% of the people interviewed about having large families were in favor of it, or in favor of them. Uh, then in 1945 it was up to 49% uh, of, of those who've *favored* having large families. This is about the time when my, my parents got started on their large family, OK? Then notice it, by 1957 there was a *decline* in the percentage of people who were in favor of having large families; uh, it was down to 38%. But by 1960 it was up again to 45%. Then there was another decline by 1966; it was down to 35%. Uh, two years later in 1968, it rose again to 41%. But by 1977, you'll notice there was a *sharp*, sharp decline. There was only 13% of those interviewed favored having large families. Then in 1978 there was a, a *slight* rise up to 17%. Now there are a number of *factors* which *affect* people's attitudes towards large families.

Tapescript/Unit 9

A Cracker House

3. Do you know these words?
   1. *A native.* The word "cracker" refers to a native of the Deep South. *A native.*
   2. *Form.* It exemplifies the concept that form follows function. *Form.*
   3. *Function.* It exemplifies the concept that form follows function. *Function.*
   4. *An attic.* There is not an attic. *An attic.*
   5. *Elements.* All of these elements are related. *Elements.*
   6. *The environment.* They are related to the environment in which the houses are located. *The environment.*
   7. *An adaptation.* It is an adaptation to very warm weather. *An adaptation.*
   8. *A manifestation.* The cracker house is a manifestation of southern culture. *A manifestation.*

In looking at your sketch of what is called the "cracker" house, uh, several things should be emphasized. First of all, the word "cracker" refers to *a native*, particularly of the Deep South. And one of the interesting things is that **crackers have developed a kind of architecture that exemplifies the concept that, uh, *form* follows *function*.** Notice, uh, several features about the house. First of all, the very high roof, uh, under which, in most cases, there is not *an attic*. The extended porch that, uh, goes all the way around the house. And the height of the house above the ground level. Now all of these *elements* are related to, uh, *the environment*, uh, in which the houses are located. Again, in the Deep

South, uh, with *an adaptation* primarily to very, very warm weather. The high roof and the porch enable the, uh, residents of the house to be as cool as possible in the many, many months of hot weather. Also, the, uh, roof overhang, uh, provides protection against, uh, the rain. The porch is sometimes called the sleeping porch. Again, in the hot weather, uh, uh, people would sleep out on these porches. The height above the ground level is interesting too. It provides for air circulation underneath of the house, but also discourages, uh, many of, uh, the creatures of nature—varmints as they're frequently called, uh, particularly snakes and insects and so on. So the cracker house is, uh, a very interesting aspect of, uh, southern culture. And, again, uh, is *a manifestation* of how the people developed a kind of architecture that would give them satisfactory housing under the, uh, weather conditions, uh, of the south-lands.

Tapescript/Unit 10

Immigration to Hawaii

3. Do you know these words?

1. *Unique.*   The educational system in Hawaii is fairly unique. *Unique.*

2. *In that.*   We're fairly unique in that our educational system is at the state level. *In that.*

3. *At the state level.*   We're fairly unique in that our educational system is at the state level. *At the state level.*

4. *Rather than.*   The educational system is at the state level rather than the city level. *Rather than.*

5. *Nonnative speaking immigrants.*   We have one of the largest percentages of nonnative speaking immigrants. *Nonnative speaking immigrants.*

6. *Broad.*   The immigrants to Hawaii have been divided into broad groups. *Broad.*

7. *Category.*   The Koreans are in the second category. *Category.*

8. *Catch-all category.*   The catch-all category has rather a lot of people. *Catch-all category.*

9. *What are the implications of these statistics?*   Now, what are the implications of these statistics for the child sitting in the classroom? *What are the implications of these statistics?*

Hawaii has a number of special problems in the area of education. We're fairly *unique in that* we have a, an educational system that is *at the state level rather than* the city or the county level. We have one of the largest percentages of *nonnative speaking immigrants,* compared to our population size, and a very large percentage of our students attend private rather than public schools. Uh, if we take a look at some numbers, uh, for example, let's look at the number of immigrants during the 19-, during the 70s, the immigrants here to Hawaii have been divided into six *broad* groups. The largest number from the Philippines, 38,389 and, uh, the second, in, in, the second *category* are the Koreans with 11,239. Japanese 4700. Uh, people from the People's Republic of China and the Republic of China were 4618. Nine hundred twenty-one Canadians and, in the *catch-all category,* others, 11,852 people. Now *what are the implications of these statistics* for the child sitting in the classroom?

Tapescript/Unit 11

The Demographic Transition

3. Do you know these words?
    1. *Demographers.* Demographers study the changing numbers of people who live and die. *Demographers.*
    2. *The birth rate.* The birth rate tells about the number of people who are born. *The birth rate.*
    3. *The death rate.* The death rate tells about the number of people who die. *The death rate.*
    4. *The demographic pattern.* The demographic pattern is predictable. *The demographic pattern.*
    5. *A nation is developing.* When a nation's developing, both the birth rate and death rate are high. *A nation is developing.*
    6. *The health care practices.* What are the health care practices in that country? *The health care practices.*
    7. *Survive.* They help people survive into old age. *Survive.*
    8. *Dramatically.* The death rate fell quite dramatically. *Dramatically.*
    9. *Transition.* What is the third stage of this demographic transition? *Transition.*

Demographers, people who study the changing numbers of people who live and die in certain areas, talk about, uh, the relationship of the number of people who are born to the number of people who die—*the birth rate* and *the death rate*. Uh, **the demographic pattern is pretty predictable in developing nations** as we've been studying. When *a nation's*, uh, *developing*, generally speaking both the birth rate and the death rate are high. They don't have very good medicine. They don't have a lot of food. And generally *the health care practices* don't, uh, make people *survive* into old age. Well, after the introduction of, of these things—new medicine and new, uh, foods and, and other health practices—generally people stop dying at the same rate. The death rate falls in the second stage quite *dramatically*, but the birth rate stays pretty high as well. In the last stage, the, the third stage of this demographic *transition*, uh, both the birth rate and the death rate are fairly low. As people become healthier, as they have more education, uh, generally, uh, you can see this, this pattern of, uh, lower birth and lower death rates.

Tapescript/Unit 12

The Advantages of Exporting

3. Do you know these words?

   1. *Summarize.* I would like to summarize some of the advantages. *Summarize.*

   2. *Advantages.* I would like to summarize some of the advantages. *Advantages.*

   3. *New market opportunities.* Let's talk about the notion of having new market opportunities. *New market opportunities.*

   4. *Customers.* It is important to find more customers. *Customers.*

   5. *The life, the recognition, and the acceptance of the company's products.* The life, the recognition, and the acceptance of the company's products can be experienced over a longer period of time. *The life, the recognition, and the acceptance of the company's products.*

   6. *Corporate growth.* The company can experience corporate growth. *Corporate growth.*

   7. *Production schedules.* The company can lengthen its production schedules. *Production schedules.*

   8. *Production resources.* The company can utilize its production resources. *Production resources.*

9. *Personnel.* The company should plan for the use of its personnel. *Personnel.*

We've been talking about, uh, developing exports for relatively small businesses. **And now I'd like to _summarize_ some of the _advantages_ for small businesses getting into the export business.** First of all, uh, the general notion of, uh, having *new market opportunities.* That is, being able to sell, uh, products to people in foreign countries, uh, to find more *customers* who'll be more attracted to the various products of the company. These two advantages are also, uh, extended by the notion that, uh, *the life, the recognition, and the acceptance of the company's products* can be experienced over a significantly longer period of time. Uh, another distinct advantage is that with the expansion into foreign market, the company itself can experience *corporate growth*, can expand its own investment and financing opportunities. And then a fifth advantage, is that, uh, the company can plan much more efficiently to lengthen its *production schedules*, to utilize its, uh, *production resources* in a much more efficient, uh, manner and plan effectively for the use of its *personnel* to produce and to market, uh, their products.

Tapescript/Unit 13

Government Expenditures

3. Do you know these words?
   1. *Government expenditures.* This pie chart shows the U.S. government expenditures. *Government expenditures.*
   2. *The current budget.* These are the government expenditures in the current budget. *The current budget.*
   3. *Direct payments to individuals.* This category shows direct payments to individuals. *Direct payments to individuals.*
   4. *National defense.* This category shows the percentage that goes to national defense. *National defense.*
   5. *Direct grants.* States and cities get direct grants. *Direct grants.*
   6. *Interest payments.* This is the percentage used for interest payments. *Interest payments.*
   7. *The leftover category.* The smallest category is the leftover category. *The leftover category.*
   8. *The current administration.* The current administration is planning to balance the budget. *The current administration.*

9. *Balance the budget.* The current administration is planning to balance the budget. *Balance the budget.*

10. *Make any cuts.* The current administration is not going to make any cuts. *Make any cuts.*

Professor, uh, **there are five categories of *government expenditures* in *the current budget.*** According to my statistics, 42% of our tax dollars go to *direct payments to individuals,* 27% to *national defense,* 12% goes to states and cities in *direct grants,* and 11% of our tax dollar is eaten up in *interest payments,* with 8% in *the leftover category.* Uh, can you explain how *the current administration* is planning to *balance the budget* when they are not going to *make any cuts*? In fact, they're planning on raising the percentage of monies that we spend on national defense, which will in turn raise our interest payments, and they are not going to collect any additional taxes. Now how are we going to handle this situation?

Tapescript/Unit 14

Ecosystems

3. Do you know these words?

1. *An interrelated system.* An ecosystem is an interrelated system. *An interrelated system.*

2. *Made up of.* It's made up of a community of animals, plants, and bacteria. *Made up of.*

3. *A community.* It's made up of a community of animals, plants, and bacteria. *A community.*

4. *A cycle of life.* An ecosystem is a cycle of life. *A cycle of life.*

5. *Pool of nutrients.* The starting point in the ecosystem is the pool of nutrients. *Pool of nutrients.*

6. *Enable.* These are minerals that enable plants to grow. *Enable.*

7. *Herbivores.* In the cycle of life there are plants and also herbivores. *Herbivores.*

8. *Exotic.* Panda bears and koalas are sometimes considered exotic. *Exotic.*

9. *Counterparted with.* Herbivores are counterparted with carnivores. *Counterparted with.*

10. *Carnivores.* Herbivores are counterparted with carnivores. *Carnivores.*

11. *Decay organisms.* When all of these plants and animals die, they become decay organisms. *Decay organisms.*

OK, the question, did everyone hear that? The, the question was what exactly is an ecosystem. Well, an ecosystem is, uh, **an ecosystem is an interrelated system made up of a community** of animals, plants, and **bacteria.** Now I'll just explain just exactly what that means. It really, what it is, is *a cycle of life,* and it's things that are all going on at the same time really. You have a starting point, and, and the starting point is the *pool of nutrients* and, uh, these are minerals that *enable* plants to grow, OK, so you have that. You also have the plants, OK. Uh, in the same cycle you have plant-eating animals, these are called *herbivores.* These include such *exotic* animals as panda bears and koalas, which I particularly like. Uh, they, uh,—those are also pu-, uh, *counterparted with* meat-eating animals, uh, *carnivores,* in other words. Uh, animals such as lions and tigers (ahem), and of course these animals eat the poor herbivores. Uh, there're also other meat-eating animals, and these other meat-eating animals eat the other meat eaters. Uh, and sometimes man is among this group, not always the most pleasant place to be. Uh, and finally what happens with all of these, these animals and plants is that when they die, they become what we call *decay organisms.* And all of these decay organisms go back into this pool of nutrients. So really what we have is a thing where out of death you have life that is formed. Uh, and so, you know, that really is, is what an ecosystem is. And, uh, I guess now, oh let's see, where was I?

Tapescript/Unit 15

International Student Survey

3. Do you know these words?
   1. *A survey form.* There's a survey form on the overhead projector. *A survey form.*
   2. *Categories.* There are eight categories on the form. *Categories.*
   3. *Listed in rank order.* The categories are listed in rank order. *Listed in rank order.*
   4. *Adjustment problems.* This chart shows how international

students rank the adjustment problems to American study. *Adjustment problems.*

5. *Meeting financial expenses.* Meeting financial expenses was ranked at number one. *Meeting financial expenses.*

6. *Budgeting time.* Budgeting time was ranked near the top. *Budgeting time.*

7. *Get involved in campus activities.* Whether to get involved in campus activities and how much to get involved in campus activities was ranked number four. *Get involved in campus activities.*

8. *Studying efficiently.* Studying efficiently was ranked number five. *Studying efficiently.*

9. *A critical thinker.* Becoming a critical thinker was ranked number six. *A critical thinker.*

10. *An independent thinker.* Becoming an independent thinker was ranked number six. *An independent thinker.*

11. *The ERIC system.* This survey was reported in the ERIC system. *The ERIC system.*

OK, I've just put up *a* rather simple *survey form* on the overhead, can you all see that? There in the middle are eight *categories* and, uh, those categories, uh, are *listed in rank order.* With the rank along the left-hand side and then, uh, it's . . . the rank order is one through eight and then the, uh, percentages on the right-hand side. Let me go through those categories to make sure that you can read them because, uh, the print is not as, uh, clear as it could be.

Ranked at number one, uh, uh, wh- what we have here first of all is **international students, uh, rank the *adjustment problems* to American study**, and ranked at number one was *meeting financial expenses* at 24%. And then at number two, *budgeting time* was at 14%. Ranked at number three, earning satisfactory grades, that was ranked at 13%. Uh, at number four, deciding whether and how much to *get involved in campus activities*, that was at 13%. Ranked at number five, *studying efficiently* at 10%. At number six, becoming a *critical* and *independent thinker* at 9%. And at number seven, selecting a field of study, that was at 8%. And ranked at number eight, meeting and knowing other students, that was at 6%. Now this survey was taken at the University of Maryland and has been reported in *the ERIC system* and, uh, this particular survey really doesn't have anything specific to do with international students. So you could take the same survey and administer it to any group of college students that you'd want to. In fact, uh, that's what I'd like you to do.

Tapescript/Unit 16

Jobs for Women and Men

3. Do you know these words?
    1. *Make that statement.* I don't really understand how you can make that statement. *Make that statement.*
    2. *Decade.* Things have changed for women in the last decade or two. *Decade.*
    3. *Table.* Take a look at the table in the textbook. *Table.*
    4. *In managerial positions.* There are more men who were in managerial positions. *In managerial positions.*
    5. *Whereas.* Whereas, there were few women who were in managerial positions. *Whereas.*
    6. *Occupied.* Few of those positions were occupied by women. *Occupied.*
    7. *Distressing.* Here is an even more distressing statistic. *Distressing.*
    8. *Statistic.* Here is an even more distressing statistic. *Statistic.*
    9. *Production supervisors.* There were not many women working as production supervisors. *Production supervisors.*
    10. *Assemblers.* Almost the same number of men and women worked as assemblers. *Assemblers.*
    11. *Down at the bottom of the heap.* Down at the bottom of the heap, most of the elementary school teachers were females. *Down at the bottom of the heap.*
    12. *The only conclusion we can draw.* This is the only conclusion we can draw from these statistics. *The only conclusion we can draw.*
    13. *Occupational positions of authority.* Occupational positions of authority continue to be dominated by males. *Occupational positions of authority.*
    14. *Dominated.* Occupational positions of authority continue to be dominated by males. *Dominated.*

Uh, well, professor, I don't, I don't really see how you can *make that statement.* I agree that things have changed for women in the last *decade* or two but, uh, if we just take a look at this *table* in our book. We see that, uh, in the 19, in 1980 there were 3,824,609 men who were *in managerial positions. Whereas* only 26.9% of the managerial positions were *occupied* by women. Uh, an even more *distressing statistic* is, uh, the, those for *production supervisors.* Fifteen percent were female, whereas there were 1,605,489 men in those positions. *Assemblers,* there were 858,542 men, 49.5% women. Cooks, 578,320 men, 57.2% were women. And then *down at the bottom of the heap,* 75.4% of all the elementary school teachers were females. There are only 569,823 male elementary school teachers in the whole country. I think *the only conclusion we can draw* from these statistics is that **the *occupational positions of authority* continue to be *dominated* by males** in this society.

Tapescript/Unit 17

USA Today

3. Do you know these words?
   1. *Edited.* USA TODAY is edited in Arlington, Virginia. *Edited.*
   2. *Composed.* USA TODAY is composed in Arlington, Virginia. *Composed.*
   3. *Satellite.* The pages are sent by satellite to 32 print sites. *Satellite.*
   4. *Sites.* The pages are sent by satellite to 32 print sites. *Sites.*
   5. *Facsimile machines.* It's made possible through the advanced technologies of facsimile machines. *Facsimile machines.*
   6. *Laser scanners.* It's made possible through the advanced technologies of laser scanners. *Laser scanners.*
   7. *The equator.* The satellite is located 22,300 miles above the equator. *The equator.*
   8. *High resolution.* The pages are placed on a high-resolution laser scanner. *High resolution.*
   9. *Laser beam.* A laser beam scans the page. *Laser beam.*
   10. *Scans.* A laser beam scans the page. *Scans.*
   11. *Beamed.* These signals are beamed to the satellite. *Beamed.*
   12. *Antenna.* Each print site has an antenna. *Antenna.*
   13. *Exposes the film.* A laser beam exposes the film. *Exposes the film.*
   14. *Processed.* The film is processed. *Processed.*
   15. *Plate.* A metal printing plate is produced. *Plate.*

So as you can see, USA TODAY is *edited* and *composed* in Arlington, Virginia, and the pages are sent by *satellite* to 32 print *sites* all around the USA. You might ask how this daily newspaper gets all around the country; well, it's made possible through the advanced technologies of *facsimile machines, laser scanners,* and Contel ASC-1 satellite, which is located 22,300 miles above *the equator.*

In Arlington, the pages are photographed and placed on a *high-resolution* laser scanner. A *laser beam scans* the page and converts the information into tiny electronic signals. At the speed of light, these signals are *beamed* to the satellite, which in turn beams the signals down to each print site simultaneously.

Each print site has an *antenna* and facsimile equipment to receive the electronic signals. The signals are sent to a computer that converts them to a laser beam that *exposes the film* and produces a full-page negative. The film is *processed* and a metal printing *plate* is produced. From this plate the four-color pages of USA TODAY are printed.

So you can see that **without this modern technology, it would be impossible for** USA TODAY **to be a national daily newspaper.**

Tapescript/Unit 18

Adjusting to College Life

3. Do you know these words?
    1. *On this campus.* It's a pleasure to meet with our new foreign students on this campus. *On this campus.*
    2. *Reassure you.* I want to reassure you about the adjustment problems that you're probably all experiencing now. *Reassure you.*
    3. *Adjustment problems.* I want to reassure you about the adjustment problems that you're probably all experiencing now. *Adjustment problems.*
    4. *Academic problems.* Some of the academic problems may be related to English. *Academic problems.*
    5. *Signed up for.* You may have accidentally signed up for the wrong courses. *Signed up for.*
    6. *Registration.* You may have accidentally signed up for the wrong courses at registration. *Registration.*
    7. *Everything was filled.* Maybe everything was filled and you had to take courses you didn't want. *Everything was filled.*

8. *Term papers.* You might be having problems writing term papers. *Term papers.*

9. *Personal problems.* Some of the personal problems may be related to loneliness. *Personal problems.*

10. *Miserable.* There was a girl crying about how miserable she was. *Miserable.*

11. *Dorm.* Maybe the dorm is so noisy you can't study. *Dorm.*

12. *Social problems.* You may have social problems because you may have problems making new friends. *Social problems.*

13. *Eventually.* Eventually all these problems are going to be taken care of. *Eventually.*

14. *Work out.* Eventually all these problems will work out. *Work out.*

15. *Struggling.* You just have to keep on struggling. *Struggling.*

16. *Overwhelming.* If it all seems too overwhelming, please come see me. *Overwhelming.*

Thank you. It's a pleasure to be here today to meet with our new foreign students *on this campus* to discuss life at our school. Uh, I want to take this opportunity to *reassure you*, uh, about the *adjustment problems* that you're probably all experiencing now. And my assurance, reassurance is this: **All international students**, uh, no matter where they come from, **have some adjustment problems while studying here**. In fact you might even say that it's normal to have problems and if you don't have problems, you may not be normal. Uh, ahem, you'll, I think you're going to find that probably most of your problems can be, uh, divided into three types. Uh, and you may have all of these or you may have some of them.

Uh, these include *academic problems*, uh, you may have accidentally *signed up for* the wrong courses at *registration* or maybe *everything was filled* and you had to take courses you didn't want. Uh, you may be having problems with English, uh, or with just generally knowing how to study properly so that you can do well on, on exams and so on. Uh, you might be having problems writing terms, *term papers.* Uh, so those are some of the academic problems.

Personal problems of course, uh, there's loneliness of course. Last, last week I had a girl crying in my office about how, how *miserable* she was, that she wanted to go home, and, uh, all that, and you know, just very sad. Uh, sometimes they're not quite as sad as that, there, there may be just a problem in the *dorm* that it's so noisy that you can't study, you can't think, you never have any peace. And, uh, of course if you try to get out of the dorm you can go apartment hunting. You may find that, find that apartments are too expensive, uh, they're too far away or the landlords won't rent to students or maybe he doesn't like foreign students or whatever. So, uh, those are all kinds of, of personal problems that might be affecting you and I'm sure you recognize some of them.

There's also *social problems* because of course most of you probably don't have all of your friends from your homeland here and, uh, you may have problems making new friends, you know, among the students that are, that are here. And, of course, there's, uh, you might also be deciding, well, I want to start dating and you might be having dating problems as well.

Uh, and, what I wanted to talk to you about basically is that *eventually* all these problems are going to be, are going to be taken care of, they will *work out.* You just have to keep on *struggling,* and if it all seems too *overwhelming,* please come see me or any of the other foreign student advisors. We're really here to help you.

Tapescript/Unit 19

Recycling Waste Water

3. Do you know these words?
   1. *Environment.* We've been studying how to protect the environment. *Environment.*
   2. *Recycle.* It's important to recycle waste materials. *Recycle.*
   3. *Waste materials.* It's important to recycle waste materials. *Waste materials.*
   4. *Otherwise.* It's important to recycle waste materials that could otherwise pollute the environment. *Otherwise.*
   5. *Pollute.* It's important to recycle waste materials that could otherwise pollute the environment. *Pollute.*
   6. *Schemes.* We've seen some recycling schemes. *Schemes.*
   7. *Industrial processes.* Industrial processes sometimes produce waste products. *Industrial processes.*
   8. *Methane gas.* Waste water can be made to produce methane gas. *Methane gas.*
   9. *Bacteria.* The process of change involves bacteria in a tank. *Bacteria.*
   10. *An anaerobic process.* The tank has no air, so this is an anaerobic process. *An anaerobic process.*
   11. *Nutrients.* The waste water has nutrients that the bacteria can feed on. *Nutrients.*

12. *Feed on.* The waste water has nutrients that the bacteria can feed on. *Feed on.*

13. *Filter.* It takes four or five hours for the water to filter up. *Filter.*

14. *Blanket.* There's a blanket of bacteria in the middle of the tank. *Blanket.*

15. *Outlet.* Clear water is taken off through one outlet. *Outlet.*

16. *Sewage treatment plant.* The water is sent on to the sewage treatment plant. *Sewage treatment plant.*

17. *Receives further purification.* The water receives further purification there. *Receives further purification.*

In the past couple weeks we've been studying how to protect the *environment* and how to *recycle waste materials* that, uh, could *otherwise pollute* the environment. We've seen some recycling *schemes*, uh, especially those that have to do with industries and the waste products that such *industrial processes*, uh, produce.

Many industries use a lot of water, of course, so it becomes important to, uh, recycle water if at all possible. We have today an example of a beer company that uses a lot of water in its processes. **The beer company that we're looking at changes waste water into *methane gas* and clear water.** It does that through a . . . a process involving bacteria, *bacteria* in a large tank. The tank doesn't have any air in it so this is an . . . *an anaerobic process.* But the waste water from the beer-making process enters at the bottom of the tank. It's full of *nutrients* and other materials that the bacteria can *feed on.* That's a slow process. It takes maybe four or five hours for the water to *filter* up through the layer of bacteria, this *blanket* of bacteria in the middle of the tank. But after that time, we've got two products. We've got clear water that is taken off through one *outlet* of the tank, and we have methane gas which is taken off out of another outlet in the tank. That methane gas can be shipped back to the . . . the beer company for them to use again for heating. Then the clear water can be sent on to the *sewage treatment plant*, uh, where it *receives further purification* and can be used again for industrial uses or even, uh, as pure drinking water.

Tapescript/Unit 20

The Scientific Method

3. Do you know these words?

1. *Our formal course.* Before we begin our formal course, I'd like to discuss the scientific method. *Our formal course.*

2. *Getting a grip on.*   We need to start out with really getting a grip on the scientific method. *Getting a grip on.*

3. *Distinct.*   There are five distinct steps within the scientific method. *Distinct.*

4. *Define a problem.*   First you need to define a problem. *Define a problem.*

5. *Throw one out.*   You always start with a question, so let's throw one out. *Throw one out.*

6. *Figure out.*   You might be interested in trying to figure out why you're not getting good grades. *Figure out.*

7. *Review the literature.*   You need to go back and take a look at what has been done in this area, so you review the literature. *Review the literature.*

8. *Formulate a hypothesis.*   The next step would be to formulate a hypothesis. *Formulate a hypothesis.*

9. *Analyze.*   You need to collect and analyze your data. *Analyze.*

10. *Data.*   You need to collect and analyze your data. *Data.*

11. *Conduct a survey.*   Another way to collect data would be to conduct a survey. *Conduct a survey.*

12. *Conclusion.*   Finally you would analyze the data and develop a conclusion. *Conclusion.*

13. *Put us on to.*   The information we find when looking at data would put us on to ideas for further research. *Put us on to.*

14. *Research.*   The information we find when looking at data would put us on to ideas for further research. *Research.*

15. *Study.*   A study always leads to more investigation. *Study.*

16. *Investigation.*   A study always leads to more investigation. *Investigation.*

All right class, before we begin, uh, *our formal course*, what I'd like to present to you, uh, is the steps in the scientific method, since this is an experimental course in psychology, uh, we need to start out with really *getting a grip on* the scientific method. **There are five *distinct* steps within the scientific method.**

First you need to *define a problem.* In a sense, you always start with some type of a question. And let's *throw one out.* How's about, uh, you might be interested in trying to *figure out* why you're not getting good grades, that's a problem. So let's put that out as, uh, the question to look at.

Now that you have the problem, the next step would be to find out who may have this problem as well and what may be some of the reasons why students aren't getting good grades. In other words, you need to go back and take a look at what has been done in this area, so you *review the literature.*

After reviewing the literature, the next step would be to *formulate a hypothesis.* And your hypothesis is going to be your working question that you can really do and collect some information to prove or disprove, uh, your hypothesis. In this case, let's say that you formed the hypothesis that the reason you're getting poor grades is because your teachers really don't care for you.

Well, now that you have your working problem, you need to collect and *analyze* your *data.* There are one of two ways you can do an experiment. Another way would be to *conduct a survey.* And in this form what you'd do is you'd interview a lot of people and gather information.

Now, now based on the data you collected through an experiment or a survey, you'd analyze it and develop a *conclusion.*

Uh, at any rate the finding that we receive from looking at the data would really *put us on to* ideas for further *research* and really in exper-, experimental psychology, or in any experiment, uh, a *study* always leads to more *investigation.* In other words, ideas for further research. All right, let's move on.

Tapescript/Unit 21

Persuasion in Speaking

3. Do you know these words?
    1. *Invent.* Aristotle did not invent rhetoric. *Invent.*
    2. *Compile.* What Aristotle did was to compile information into a book. *Compile.*
    3. *Encounter.* Each speaking encounter is different. *Encounter.*
    4. *Gruesome.* You can give gruesome examples. *Gruesome.*
    5. *Colleague.* Gary is my colleague. *Colleague.*
    6. *Ethnicity.* Part of my ethos is my ethnicity. *Ethnicity.*
    7. *Superficial.* It's a superficial kind of thing. *Superficial.*
    8. *Component.* How you dress is one component of ethos. *Component.*
    9. *Slick.* She gave a memorized, slick presentation. *Slick.*
    10. *Impediment.* He has a speech impediment. *Impediment.*
    11. *Analysis.* Content analysis is worth 45%. *Analysis.*
    12. *Frosting.* Language is the frosting in a speech. *Frosting.*

13. *Crucial.*   Knowing about ethos is crucial. *Crucial.*

14. *Valid.*   What Aristotle said in ancient times is valid today. *Valid.*

. . . So let me begin with the first man that I want to introduce you to. He is the Father of Rhetoric. He may be the father of some other subject that you've studied, but Aristotle is the Father of Rhetoric. He's the father of many things, and that's because he is a . . . an organizer of information. He did not *invent* rhetoric, but what he did is take all existing information at that time and *compile* it into a very readable, understandable book. Aristotle defined rhetoric as the art of deciding in the particular case, each particular case, what are the available means of persuasion. That means that he saw all public speaking as persuasion. And I think that you probably would agree with him if you thought about it. And if you realize that if you give a speech to inform—basically today we say there're three types of speeches: inform, persuade, entertain—if you give a speech to inform, then in fact you are persuading the audience that what you're informing them about is important. What I'm giving you today is a speech to inform. Right? So let's give Aristotle the fact that public speaking is persuasion. And if you give him that, then **he says there are basically three types of persuasion.** And you have to decide in a particular case which . . . how you are going to use these three, because you're going to use them differently depending on each speaking *encounter*. Now I'm going to define these two more times for you. Literally, "ethos" can be defined as ethical appeal. "Pathos" as pathetic. And "logos" as logical. And I'll take it a step further because that can be confusing, and we will say that when we're talking about ethos, we're talking about a speaker's credibility. Pathos is appeal to emotions, and logos is appeal to reason. And the most important of these three? Do you know? Well, I'll tell you what Aristotle wanted it to be. He wanted it to be reason. He thought the most important thing you can do when you're giving a speech is be reasonable. And you don't want it to be emotional. Right? You don't want the most important thing you can bring to a speech is whether or not you can talk about how bloody something was or how . . . give *gruesome* examples or wonderful examples. The most important one is ethos. So we've got to talk about that more than we have to talk about the other two.

What makes up your credibility? And can you do anything about it? Are you stuck with your ethos? Well, when I came in here to speak to you, those of you who know me, then I have some ethos, good or bad, based on your knowledge of me. Andrew is my student. I've met you once. Gary is my *colleague*. So you have some sort of opinion of me. That's part of my ethos. It comes in with me when I begin speaking. For those of you who don't know me at all, part of my ethos is my sex, my age, what I'm wearing, what I look like, my *ethnicity*. And I can't do a lot about . . . I can do a lot about what I look like. Can't do much about my age, my sex, and my *ethnicity*. So that's a given. But that's part of my ethos. So when we talk about how can you deal with influencing your ethos . . . well, one thing you can do—and it's a *superficial* kind of thing, but it's important is that you can decide what you're going to wear that will be appropriate to the audience. So that and what is appropriate doesn't . . . very is very much determined by the audience. It's one *component* of, of ethos that you can adjust. What else can you manipulate, deal with? Well, another important *component* of ethos is whether or not you are well prepared and organized. If you are disorganized and you come in and you look good, you've got a good background, you're dressed right, and you come in and you keep saying, "Oh, gee, I'm sorry but I left that in the other room" and "Oh, I didn't really mean to say this point right now" and lots "ah's" and "uh's" . . . you can destroy the good credibility that you came in with by poor organization and being unprepared. Also, if I came in to speak to you, just think about this, what if I came in to talk to you about classical rhetoric and how important it is to my field of public speaking and I gave it to you like this: "And next we want to talk about Aristotle's da-da-da-da." You see if I don't look at you, if I read it to you, boy have I hurt my ethos! Right? If I don't look at you, do you think I know, I care about you at all? Likewise, I'm telling you something if I memorized it. If I had this so memorized that you knew, you could tell, you can tell when somebody's got it memorized. Right? And you know it's just clicking off and you can, you can almost hear the periods, and if I did that to you, and I was doing a terrific job . . . I looked good but I . . . I wasn't looking at you. I was just giving this memorized, *slick* presentation. That would hurt my ethos, not as bad as reading it to you, but almost because when you're speaking to an audience, an important element of ethos is whether or not you communicate with them. So what I'm talking about is your appearance, your organization, and your delivery. You know what's the least important? And it sure . . . this ought to be important to anybody where English is a second language. The least important thing is language. Not that you shouldn't be able to say it, but if you have an accent, people don't . . . that doesn't bother people. If you are well organized and you deliver it well, they could care about an accent. They can care if you, you know, lisp or have a speech *impediment* of some sort. They've done extensive studies and they've found out that content *analysis* is worth, let's say, 45% in terms of what makes a good speech. What you say and how you're organized—45%. Delivery—45%. Language—10%. It's the *frosting*. So you should never in terms of public speaking, you should never let an accent bother you because that's not . . . if you've got everything else. If you . . . if you've got an accent and you're disorganized and you don't look at people, they're lost, you know, they're totally lost. So it's important that you if you do have, if English is your second language, that you work really hard on organization and delivery and then . . . then don't worry about the rest. Okay, I'll leave . . . ethos is my favorite term and any student who graduates from my class better know ethos or else. It's *crucial*.

Pathos then is appeal to emotions. And how do you appeal to emotions? Let's say that you're giving a speech on child abuse. If you want to appeal to my emotions, you would . . . you would show me pictures. I wouldn't want to look. You'd show me pictures of child abuse and you would tell me examples of a poor child that was abused. That's appeal to my emotions. If you wanted to appeal to my reason, then you would give me statistics that there were so many thousand children abused. But I'll tell you if you can tell me a thousand were abused in 1983 and 10,000 are abused in 1984, my mind can't make that leap. It can just say, "Oh, it has increased." But I can't . . . I can't feel that much more pity or anger because of the numbers, but if you give me emotional appeal, then I can feel and then give me numbers. So the two have to be combined. And in every case you must make individual decisions, and the more educated your audience, the more you are going to stress what? Reason and logic. The more uneducated your audience, the more you're going to give examples and not worry so much about the numbers and statistics and so forth. But every time you speak, those three are into play, and the amazing thing about Aristotle is what he said in ancient times, classical period, is still *valid* today. You can't read this book and say, "No, no, not true anymore." Ethos, pathos, and logos—absolutely true—any speaking situation you hear today. And that's why he's the Father of Rhetoric.

Tapescript/Unit 22

The Basic Accounting Formula

3. Do you know these words?

1. *Keeping track of.*   Accounting is keeping track of stuff. *Keeping track of.*

2. *Hint.*   Let me give you a hint. *Hint.*

3. *Tool.*   The balance sheet is an accounting tool. *Tool.*

4. *Seesaw.*   The balance sheet is something like a seesaw. *Seesaw.*

5. *Accountants.*   Accountants have a fancy name for that. *Accountants.*

6. *Assets.*   The stuff that we own is called assets. *Assets.*

7. *Inventory.*   We call those products inventory. *Inventory.*

8. *Fixtures.*   We call the shelving fixtures. *Fixtures.*

9. *Tend to.* People tend to believe you. *Tend to.*

10. *Debt.* When we have credit and use it, we create a debt. *Debt.*

11. *Liabilities.* The stuff we owe is liabilities. *Liabilities.*

12. *Investment.* So here we have investment. *Investment.*

13. *Analogy.* To use our own analogy, this is stuff that's ours. *Analogy.*

14. *Equity.* Equity is a little bit like ice cream. *Equity.*

15. *Derivative of.* Derivative of this equation are two others. *Derivative of.*

Accounting is the basic language of business. Every business, no matter how large or how small, uses accounting. It doesn't matter whether it's Aloha Airlines or Longs Drugs or a steel company. It all . . . all of these businesses use accounting. Why, you ask. Why? Thank you very much, Mi Sook. Why? Because you've got to know who won. If you, did any of you watch . . . did any of you watch the basketball game last night against the Boston Celtics or the Boston Celtics against—who did they play? . . . Boston played New York. Who won? Don't know. Well, the score was 98 to 91. Who won? The 98, yeah, that's right. That's accounting. It's *keeping track of* stuff. For basketball it's *keeping track of* the number of times the ball goes through the hoop. What do you think we're going to keep track of in accounting? Not the number of times the balls goes through the hoop, but what? What do you think we're going to keep track of, Jian? You don't know. What do you think we're going to keep track of in business? Let me give you a *hint.* Money. That's what we're going to keep track of . . . money. And we're going to keep track of it in various forms. OK.

How many of you have been to Longs Drug Stores? Have you been to Longs? OK. Everybody's been to Longs. When you walk inside a Longs Drugs, what do you see? Stuff, lots of stuff. Right? OK. We're going to keep . . . one of the things we're going to do is keep track of that stuff. OK. Now where did this stuff come from? You go into Longs Drugs and you see liquor and you see shampoo and you see glasses. Where did all that stuff come from? It came from factories, so Longs bought it from someone. OK. Where did the money come from? Customers or banks. OK. Now when we start to keep track of stuff in business, we're going to use an accounting *tool* known as the balance sheet. And in your books you'll notice that the balance sheet's represented by this nice little T. And on this T . . . this T is something like a *seesaw.* Okay? In accounting it's always level. It's always even. Never up. Never down. Always level. On this side of the balance sheet (and we'll put balance sheet up here) . . . on this side of the balance sheet we're going to have stuff, things that we own. OK. *Accountants,* of course, have a fancy name for that. *Accountants* have a fancy name for everything. And all you really have to do is get the idea and then attach the fancy name to it. In some ways, this accounting course is going to be like a language course. You're going to be learning a language. We're going to put together ideas and then put labels on them. Now the stuff that we own, *accountants* call this *assets*. *Assets*—things that we own. So if you were to go into Longs Drug Store, what would be the *assets* that would be in a Longs Drug Store? Hau, name one of the *assets* that would be inside a Longs Drug Store. Kyung Hwa, anything. OK. Mi Sook says a product. All right. Now we've got a general class of things called products. In business what would we call that? In accounting we call those products . . . we call those *inventory* . . . the things that we sell.

So *inventory* would be type of an *asset*. What else is going to be in Longs Drug Store? *Fixtures*. Right. You see all the shelving that the products are sitting on. Those are *assets* as well. We call those, oddly enough, *fixtures*. Thank you, Gary. What else would be there? How about the cash registers? Those are *assets*. What's inside the cash register? Money. That's an *asset*. So all of these things are *assets*. All right. Now on the other side of the balance sheet is where these *assets* came from. Now *assets* over here, now we had to get these *assets* from someone. Now nothing comes from nothing. You look in the air and if there's nothing there, what do you have? Nothing. If we've got *assets* here, they came from one of two sources, so on the balance sheet we *tend to* split this up into two parts. Now if the *assets*, for instance, the *inventory*, if we bought that from a factory, we bought that from another business. OK.

And we didn't pay them immediately. We said, "Yes, we want to have your stuff and we promise to pay you . . . we promise that we're going to pay you." And if you're Longs Drug, people *tend to* believe you. What would we create with that promise to pay? "I promise to pay." Not a guarantee. Not a treaty. What would we . . . we say if you give me your product, I promise you to pay . . . I promise to pay you. Credit, yes. Exactly so, Sungdon. Exactly so. Credit. Now when we create credit, we also create . . . when we have credit and use it, we create a *debt*. Now if this is stuff that we own, what is a *debt*? A *debt* is stuff we owe. We owe money to these other companies. The fancy accounting name for that? Anybody know the fancy accounting name for that? Gary, do you know the fancy accounting name for the stuff that we owe? (I didn't read the chapter last night.) Take him out and have him shot. OK. The fancy accounting name for the stuff we owe is *liabilities*.

OK. The stuff we owe. We owe people *liabilities*. We are liable. We owe that. The other source . . . the other place that these *assets* can come from is from people investing in a business. People say, "I want to start up a business." And they put their money into it. And they use the money to buy stuff and then sell it. So here we have *investment*, or to use our *analogy*: this is stuff that's ours. Say we've got stuff, stuff, stuff. And we're just going to put a fancy accounting term on that. The fancy accounting term for this stuff is *equity*. *Equity* is a little bit like ice cream. *Equity* for business comes in three flavors: if only one person owns the company, OK, that's a sole proprietorship. It's called owner's *equity*. If two or more people own it, and it's a partnership, it's called . . . what would you guess? . . . partner's *equity*. Pretty good. Partner's *equity*. What if it is a corporation? A lot of people owning a business. That's what a corporation is. What would you call their *equity*? OK, it's a company.

But what do you call your part of that company? Yeah, there we go. Stock, because if you have a big company, everyone has a little part of it. You have stocks, so we call this: stockholder's *equity*. You're only going to have one of these in every company. It's either going to be a sole proprietorship with owner's *equity*, or a partnership with partner's *equity*, or a corporation with shareholder's or stockholder's *equity*. OK. This little picture right here . . . this balance sheet picture that we have gives us the basic accounting equation. OK? We're going to reduce it to very small symbols so that it's easy to remember. And we say that A, *assets*, equal what? *Liabilities* plus *equity*. **Your basic accounting equation: *Assets* equal *liabilities* plus *equity*.** For those of you who like to drink, it's easy to remember. What is this? This is ale, which is a good beer. OK. Now *derivative* of this equation are two others. Right? You could turn this equation around and get two other equations from it, couldn't you? What's another equation? A − L = E or A − E = L. Okay. Reasonable. Very reasonable set of assumptions.

Tapescript/Unit 23

Nutrition

3. Do you know these words?
   1. *Nutrients.* We talk about the six classes of nutrients. *Nutrients.*
   2. *Poultry.* Poultry is a good source of protein. *Poultry.*
   3. *Zip.* Calories give you zip and energy. *Zip.*
   4. *Function.* The main function of carbohydrates is to provide energy. *Function.*
   5. *Complex.* Rice is a complex carbohydrate. *Complex.*
   6. *Concentrated.* Fats supply energy in a concentrated form. *Concentrated.*
   7. *Calories.* Fats have a lot of calories. *Calories.*
   8. *Excess.* Excess protein will make you fat. *Excess.*

9. *Deficiency.* You must drink milk to prevent a calcium deficiency. *Deficiency.*
10. *Cheat.* You can't cheat. *Cheat.*
11. *Can't stand.* If you can't stand milk, you can take a calcium pill. *Can't stand.*
12. *Hit.* You think that way until you hit about 40. *Hit.*
13. *Osteoporosis.* They have no osteoporosis. *Osteoporosis.*
14. *Osteomalacia.* They have no osteomalacia. *Osteomalacia.*
15. *Caries.* They have no dental caries. *Caries.*

In nutrition we try to figure out the foods we need to make us fit, make us healthy. That is our goal. Eating the right foods to be healthy. Therefore, I have given you a handout. It is the pink handout, the pink handout, the simple one. I guess it's simple to talk about this in colors. Now **what we talk about all during the year are the six classes of *nutrients.*** We talk about the six classes of *nutrients.* These six classes of *nutrients* are one—protein, two—carbohydrates. (This is the way we say the word.) Three—fats. Four—minerals. Very good. Five—no, calcium is a mineral. Five is vitamins on the other side. Vitamins. And six is not on your list, but you might want to add it. It is water. Water is the sixth class of *nutrients.* We want you to have all six classes of these *nutrients* each and every day. OK?

Let's just talk a little bit about them. All of the information will be found on your pink sheets, so you won't have to take lots and lots of notes. You can follow along very easy. The first one—protein. Why do we need protein? We need proteins to build, repair, and maintain our body. For example, my hair is protein. My cheeks are protein. My fingernails are protein. My eyebrows are protein. Everything you are looking at on me is protein right now. Our body's about two-thirds water, but the next biggest thing we are probably is protein and calcium, which is a mineral. But if you look at us, we're all protein. If you notice, our hair is different, our skin is different, so we have different kinds of proteins but these are all proteins. Therefore, you need to eat a lot of protein in your diet so that you will be able to have fingernails, hairs, eyes, eyebrows, and everything. It's for growth and repair. The sources—where do we find protein in our food? Where are we going to get this thing so we can grow? The food sources, if you will notice right on your pink sheet, from the animal proteins are meat—which would be like your beef—fish, or pork. Beef or pork or lamb. Fish, *poultry*, milk, eggs, cheese. Vegetable proteins are dried beans and peas, soybeans, nuts, and tofu. OK? But these are just some of the food that you should eat every day in your diet. You don't have to eat a lot now. You don't have to go out and order yourself a one-pound steak, five fish, three dozen eggs. You don't have to eat like a piggy. Just a little bit. As a matter of fact, four ounces of protein per day is enough. So if you go to visit McDonald's and you get the Big Mac, that's enough for the day. You don't need a lot. You need lots of vegetables and fruits and just a little bit of protein. Okay?

Now, the next class of *nutrients* is the carbohydrates. The carbohydrates, if you will notice, they supply energy—energy for your activities. They're *calories*. They give you *zip* and energy to run around. That's what gives you all of your, your energy to do all of your activities. They're very, very important. They also help your body use other *nutrients*, but the main *function* of carbohydrates . . . let me just erase this. The main reason you need carbohydrates is for energy to keep yourself going. Someone told me a carbohydrate that they ate was rice. And you'll notice that's the first one listed. Rice is a *complex* carbohydrate. It is a good carbohydrate. It gives you lots of energy. Bread, cereals, potatoes—OK, I just want you to know that you only need four servings per day of that one. But you need a little bit of that. Four servings per day would be about four scoops of rice. Some of you are bigger, so six you might need.

Fats is this next class of *nutrients*. Fats supply energy in a *concentrated* form. As a matter of fact, *calories* has a lot of, or fats have a lot of *calories* in them. OK, protein has four *calories* per gram. OK? In other words now, if you eat too many proteins, it could get you fat. People, we see people who are weight lifters, you know, that lift weights, and they're drinking liquid protein. They don't understand in their head. They cannot figure it out. If you eat too much protein, you can make yourself fat. *Excess* protein will make you fat. Carbohydrates for energy. Let's put this here. We have four *calories* per gram. However, if we eat fat, you're going to be real sorry about that because fat, too much fat will also make you fat—very fat. Okay, F-A-T. Fat equals fat because look here. There are nine *calories* per gram. You see what I'm saying to you? It doesn't take long for that one to add up. And people like this one because it tastes good. That's the problem. So you see you take a look down here now. We have fats supply energy in *concentrated* form. Butter, margarine. How many of you never use butter or margarine on your bread? No, you see we like it, don't we? Oil, cream, lard, shortening, fats on meats and other things, sour cream, salad dressings, coconut, whipped cream, mayonnaise, macadamia nuts, cashew nuts. These things aren't on the list, but these are all foods that are very high in fat. Peanut butter, bacon . . . all of these things are fats. They're not protein or anything else. They're fats. You eat too many and you look just as round as a macadamia nut. It'll give you that new look very quick. OK, fats. More about this later.

OK, minerals. Your pink sheet has probably the three most important minerals as far as our diet is concerned. It's not that there aren't other important minerals, but this may well be, these three may well be the most important. Calcium, found in your bones and your teeth. That's what it's important for—bones and teeth. Makes you have strong bones and strong teeth. And I'm going to tell you something else. This is just a quick little aside . . . this is what you would call one semester of nutrition in 60 minutes. How many of you have seen people going down . . . old ladies going down the street that look like this? Anybody seen that look? Do you know how they get it? Do you know how they get it? No calcium in the diet. Long-term calcium *deficiency*. It happens to women more than it happens to men. You must absolutely, positively drink milk all of your life. You can't *cheat*. If you *cheat*, when you are old that's how you will walk down the street. Don't *cheat* on that topic. You must have milk. If you *can't stand* milk, take a look at that pink sheet I just gave you now. We have . . . calcium is found in milk, cheese, foods made of milk, small fish with bones like sardines. If you buy a can of salmon, the bones. Eat those bones in that salmon can. Don't throw them out. Dark green, leafy vegetables. Yogurt. Some legumes like white beans, garbanzo, or soy beans. If you absolutely, positively can't drink milk, won't drink milk, and won't eat any of those foods, I . . . the only pill I ever recommend you take . . . I recommend you take a calcium pill because I'm telling you you will not win in the end. In the end, if you do not drink calcium starting—or drink milk or eat calcium from today on, when you are an old lady that's how you are going to walk down the street. When you are an old man, that's how you are going to walk down the street. You can't *cheat*. You just can't *cheat*. Okay, you must get your calcium. It is very, very important. See you're young now and you're 18, 19, and 20. You've already had the chickens. You've already had the measles. You've already had all . . . I mean chicken pox, the measles, and the mumps. You've had all this stuff. You're not worried about heart disease. And you're not worried about cancer. You think you're going to live forever. Well, you think that way until you *hit* about 40. And you realize that forever is coming to an end. Then you start worrying about how you eat. Therefore, start early on. Don't wait until you're 40. You may already be humping over. You don't want that look. I don't want anybody to look that way.

Okay, the next one we have . . . there is iron. Iron is very important in the blood. Liver is the best source of iron. Oh, I'm running out of time here. Liver is the very best source of iron. You find it in other foods such as dried beans and peas, spinach, etcetera. Women have more of a problem with iron than men because they lose blood once a month during their period. But it's very important to get iron in your diet. Flourine, which is the next mineral listed necessary for strong teeth, prevents tooth decay, prevents cavities in the teeth. Makes strong bones in adults.

In some parts of the country, they put fluoride in your drinking water. You just get in whether, you know, no matter what. In other parts of the country it naturally occurs in the water. You can't take it out if you want to. As a matter of fact, there are three areas of the United States where it naturally occurs in the water. But it naturally occurs in the water in Texas, in Pueblo, Colorado, and near Jamestown, North Dakota in that particular area. The people there . . . they don't need a dentist. Their teeth are just really strong. In fact, if you go to those towns, those people have kind of brownish teeth. It looks like they've been chewing tobacco. We call it mottled teeth. But there's no cavities. Their teeth . . . and they have no *osteoporosis*, no *osteomalacia*, no dental *caries* . . .

Tapescript/Unit 24

The Law of Demand

3. Do you know these words?

1. *Determines.* We're going to take a look at what determines the price of a product. *Determines.*

2. *Exists.* A market exists if there is at least one buyer and one seller. *Exists.*

3. *Flea market.* A market could be a physical place like the flea market. *Flea market.*

4. *Motivated.* Buyers and sellers are motivated by different forces. *Motivated.*

5. *Forces.* Buyers and sellers are motivated by different forces. *Forces.*

6. *Afford.* That's all that you need and can afford. *Afford.*

7. *Factor.* Another important factor is the price of related goods. *Factor.*

8. *Purchasing patterns.* There are many factors that influence your purchasing patterns. *Purchasing patterns.*

9. *Isolate.* We isolate one key variable. *Isolate.*

10. *Key.* We isolate one key variable. *Key.*

11. *Variable.* We isolate one key variable. *Variable.*

12. *Determinant.* The price is the key determinant of your decision. *Determinant.*

This morning we're going to talk about how a market works. We observe every day you go into the store to buy things . . . you buy things at different prices and you observe that some those prices rise, and so today we're going to take a look at what *determines* the price of a product. And why is it that the prices of certain products go up while the prices of other products go down. Now the U.S. economy is primarily what we call a market economy. A market is an institution . . . a mechanism whereby two groups of people, buyers and sellers, interact to exchange information and exchange goods and services. Now a market *exists* if there is at least one buyer and one seller and this exchange can take place between the buyer and the seller. A buyer . . . a market could be a physical place like the *flea market* at Aloha Stadium, or it could be a place like the New York Stock Exchange where ownership claims to the corporations . . . stocks are bought and sold. Now buyers and sellers behave in different ways and they're *motivated* by different *forces*. Now I'm going to ask you to think a minute and pretend that you are going into the store to buy something . . . chicken, maybe. OK? **What *motivates* you to buy that chicken?** What are the *forces* that influences your behavior? Economists have observed buyers buying things over the last 500 years. What's the *key*? . . . What is it? You might buy chicken because you like chicken, huh? Right? As opposed to beef or . . . huh? It's good for you. It's good for you, huh? You know, one . . . you might like chicken, you have a taste or preference for chicken. You prefer chicken over beef. You prefer chicken over drumsticks or . . . huh? What else? Why is it that you buy . . . let's say chicken costs 99 cents a pound. Why is it that you only buy five pounds of chicken and not ten pounds? Or 15 pounds? That's all that you need and can *afford*. Right? For another important *factor* is how much income you have . . . how much income you have. OK? The more income you have, the more chicken you can buy. Right? The less income you have, the less chicken you can buy. So you like chicken. You have a taste or preference for chicken and you can *afford* to buy that chicken. OK? Another important *factor* is the prices of related goods. By related goods we mean substitutes, substitutes, substitute goods. A substitute good is a good that can be used in the place of another good. So instead of buying chicken, you could have purchased beef. The price of beef will influence how much chicken you buy. The more expensive beef is, the less chicken you will buy or the more chicken you would buy. Right? The more expensive beef is, the more chicken you would buy because you can't *afford* to buy the beef so you buy the chicken instead. OK? Another related good are goods that we call complementary goods. Complementary goods are goods that are used together. They complement each other. OK? Complementary goods. Can you think of a good that is complementary to chicken? You buy some chicken . . . let's say you want to make barbequed chicken. You would need to buy the chicken and the barbeque sauce. Right? The barbeque sauce is a complementary good. It is used together with the chicken . . . a complementary good. If the price of complementary goods increase or decrease, this is going to affect how much chicken you buy . . . complementary goods. So we look at the prices of these related goods—the prices of substitute goods and the prices of complementary goods—because they will influence . . . the prices of these goods will influence how much chicken you will buy.

Can you think of other *factors*, other *factors* that influence how much chicken you buy? What if the price of chicken had gone up to ten dollars a pound? What would happen? Would you buy more or less? Less. So one *key factor* is the price, the price of the good itself. The more expensive it is, the higher the price, the less you buy. The less you buy. The price of the good, your taste or preference for the good, your income, the price of related goods, all of these *determine* how much you buy. Now in looking at all of these *factors*, economists, you know, there are many, many *factors* that influence . . . right . . . your *purchasing patterns*, your decision to buy chicken. Of all of these *factors*, we *isolate* one *key variable*, one *key factor*. Of all of these *factors* the most important *factor*, we have observed, is the price, the price. Of all of these *factors*, the price is the *key determinant* of your decision to buy chicken. In fact, economists have observed that the higher the price, the less chicken people will buy. The lower the price of chicken, the more chicken people will buy. And this we call the law of demand. The law of demand describes how consumers react . . . right . . . to a change in price.

Tapescript/Unit 25

The Judicial System

3. Do you know these words?
   1. *Arson.* A felony is a serious crime like murder or arson. *Arson.*
   2. *Embezzlement.* A felony is a serious crime like kidnapping or embezzlement. *Embezzlement.*
   3. *Violate.* In order to arrest a person, the person must violate a criminal law. *Violate.*
   4. *Preliminary.* In ten days we will have a preliminary hearing. *Preliminary.*
   5. *Sufficient.* There is sufficient evidence to indicate a crime has been committed. *Sufficient.*
   6. *Plead.* The man who stole the money with the gun will plead guilty. *Plead.*
   7. *Verdict.* The clerk of the court will take the verdict from the jury foreman. *Verdict.*
   8. *Defendant.* We find the defendant guilty. *Defendant.*
   9. *Penitentiary.* A felony will mean at least a year in the penitentiary. *Penitentiary.*

10. *Impose sentence.* On June 30 the judge will impose sentence. *Impose sentence.*

What happens to a person when they are arrested for a felony offense? Now before we start, a felony means a serious crime like murder, robbery, burglary, *arson*, rape, *embezzlement*, kidnapping. Those are felonies.

All right, here is basically how this system operates of ours. First of all, we have the legislature. Then, before that of course, the most important—that's the people. They elect the legislature. The legislature in turn passes the laws. And for our purposes today and for any purpose actually, there are two sets of laws in America. One is civil and the other is criminal. And this is the one we're interested in today—criminal. We care not about this. OK. In order to arrest a person, the person must *violate* a criminal law. As I already have pointed out, it could be murder, robbery, burglary, those types of things. There has to be a written law which describes the conduct which our system of laws do not permit. We are not allowed in our country, or any country I know of, to go up and kill another person or to go up and put a gun in a person's side and take their money. We cannot do that. Now, we'll take a situation where a person has robbed another person. That's a very common crime in America. It's a very serious crime. But we'll take this crime as an example. A person walks up to another one on the street, puts a gun to his side, and says, "Give me your money and your watch and everything else you have." So the person gives him all his money and his belongings. He turns and runs. The person who has just been victimized will call the police. But let's just figure the police get a hold of the person and he is arrested. All right? After he is arrested, he will be taken to the jail. He will be fingerprinted. He will be photographed and personal history will be taken about him such as where he was born, his name, his mother's name, things like this. All right. Then after a certain number of days, he will be taken into court. The court is what we call inferior court. And I'll abbreviate this because I'm getting near the end of the line and I'll have to start over again. The inferior court. In the inferior court, the suspect, as he is now called, the man who did the sticking up, will be asked by the judge: "Do you have a lawyer? Do you have money for a lawyer? Do you understand why you are here? And do you have anything you want to say?" The . . . let's play like the man, the suspect says, "I have not hired a lawyer yet, but I have the money to hire one." The judge says, "All right. In ten days you will return to this courtroom and we will have a *preliminary* hearing." All right. So ten days later, and I have just made up the ten-day business because it will vary from state to state, but usually it's two weeks or a week, something like this. He will go in for *preliminary* hearing. At this time, the prosecutor, who represents the victim and also represents the people of the entire state against criminals, will put upon the witness stand the victim who will state in a very, very few words that yes, he was walking down along a certain street. A person did approach him, put a gun to his chest, and took his money. All right. And then the prosecutor will ask the victim: "Is that person in the courtroom today?" And the victim will say, "Yes, the man sitting there with the blue suit on." All right. They ask very few questions. They get it over with as quickly as possible. If the judge says, in his mind he's saying this, "There is *sufficient* evidence to indicate a crime has been committed. There is also *sufficient* evidence to indicate that this man who has been accused is the one who committed the crime. Therefore, you are held to answer." This means you must now stand trial. They go to trial, and in most cases in American jurisprudence (that means the legal process and the court system here), in most instances, this person who I've been describing, the man who stole the money with the gun, will *plead* guilty somewhere in here. Ninety percent of the cases he *pleads* guilty. So there is no trial. But in this case, the man wants a trial, so because we are allowed a trial by jury in the United States for most criminal offenses, he will demand a trial by jury. So all right, the trial starts. The case is presented to the jury and after a couple of days, the jury retires. When they say the jury retires, it doesn't mean they go on rest. They go to another room. They discuss among themselves whether or not the evidence is *sufficient* to indicate that this man did commit the crime and so on. In this case, we'll say that they agree, "Yes, he did." They come back in and the clerk of the court, which is one of the officials of the court system, will take the *verdict* from the jury foreman, the man or woman who is in charge of the other 11 jurors, and read it, then give it to the judge. The judge reads it. Then the jury foreman will say . . . he will be asked, "Have you reached a *verdict?*" "Yes, we have." "How do you find the *defendant?*" "We find him guilty." OK, so that's fine. That's what he deserved. He should be guilty. But now before the judge sentences this man to the *penitentiary*, he will do some different things. One, he will say, "You will be remanded"—that means turn back to the custody of the sheriff or the police officers—"where you will remain in jail until June 30. June 30 you will return to the courtroom and I will *impose sentence.*" The judge will then decide by the law which sentence will be imposed.

ANSWER KEY

Unit 1
Math Graduates

3. *Do You Know These Words?*

1. anxious (b)

2. majors (a)

3. statistical (c)

4. blue collar jobs (d)

5. clerical (e)

5. *Identify the Focus*

1. Just because math is your major you're not going to end up in math-related jobs. (These are the words on the tape.)

2. Since math is your major you will end up with math-related jobs. (This sentence is different in meaning from the other three sentences. Some math majors do not get jobs in math-related areas.)

3. You're not going to be doing jobs related to mathematics simply because you have a degree in math. (This sentence is similar in meaning to sentences one or four.)

4. Your major is mathematics but you will not necessarily get a job related to your major. (This sentence is similar in meaning to sentences one and three.)

6. *Making Notes: The Focus*

math maj ≠ math rel jobs

Abbreviated

major
related

Words Left Out

just, because, is, your, you're, not, going, to, end, up, in

Symbols

≠

7. Making Notes: The Supporting Details

Math-related		Not Math-related	
math/statcl jobs	13%	blue collar jobs	7%
elem/secdry tchg	12%	mgrs	7%
collg tchrs	4%	clercl jobs	16%
computr speclst	30%	serv jobs	4%
		retl sales	1%
		othr	7%

Unit 2
The Hydrologic Process

3. Do You Know These Words?

1. the hydrologic process (g)

2. evaporation (e)

3. precipitation (d)

4. aquifers (a)

5. transpiration (f)

6. atmosphere (c)

7. water vapor (b)

5. Identify the Focus

1. Evaporation and precipitation are the two parts of the hydrological process. (This sentence is similar in meaning to sentences two and three.)

2. The hydrological process is a process of evaporation and precipitation. (These are the words on the tape.)

3. The water cycle is about the change of water vapor to rain, snow, etc., and back to water again. (This sentence is similar in meaning to sentences one and two.)

4. Water has three forms: ice, water, and steam. (The fourth sentence describes water but not the hydrological cycle.)

6. _Making Notes: The Focus_

hydrologl proc = proc evap ↑ & precip ↓

Abbreviated
hydrological
process
evaporation
precipitation

Words Left Out
The, is, a, of, and

Symbols
&, ↓, ↑, =

7. _Making Notes: The Supporting Details_

prec e.g. H_2O earth   sm H_2O evap/trans—H_2O atmos
        #1   #3

H_2O vapr—clouds—rain   sm H_2O aquifr, ungrnd H_2O
        #4   #2

Unit 3
Life Expectancy

3. _Do You Know These Words?_

1. life expectancy (f)

2. column (a)

3. poorest countries (d)

4. the entire range (b)

5. categories (e)

6. the most developed countries (c)

5. _Identify the Focus_

1. Life expectancy is all the same around the world. (This sentence is different in meaning from the other three since it says that everyone, everywhere can expect to live the same number of years.)

2. Life expectancy is not the same all around the world. (These are the words that are on the tape.)

3. People everywhere on the globe are not expected to live the same number of years. (This sentence is similar in meaning to sentences two and four.)

4. People die at different ages in different countries. (This sentence is similar in meaning to sentences two and three.)

6. Making Notes: The Focus

life expectncy ≠ wrld

Abbreviated
expectancy
world

Words Left Out
is, not, the, same, all, around, the

Symbols
≠

7. Making Notes: The Supporting Details

▦	39 yrs. or less
▨	40–49 yrs.
⚃	50–59 yrs.
▨	60–69 yrs.
▦	70 yrs. +

Unit 4
World Energy Sources

3. Do You Know These Words?

1. accounts for (b)

2. energy supply (e)

3. fossil fuels (c)

4. energy source (g)

5. garbage and refuse (f)

6. at the very bottom (a)

7. that's really it (d)

5. Identify the Focus

1. Five energy sources can be found in most countries around the world. (This sentence is different from the other three sentences. The speaker does not state or imply that all sources of energy are found in most countries.)

2. There are five various energy resources on earth. (This sentence is similar in meaning to sentences three and four.)

3. The world's energy supply comes from five sources. (This sentence is similar in meaning to sentences two and four.)

4. What you have in the world is five different sorts of energy. (These are the words on the tape.)

6. Making Notes: The Focus

world energy = 5 diff sorts

Abbreviated
different

Words Left Out
what, you, have, in, the, is, of

Symbols
=

7. Making Notes: The Supporting Details

left out sol energy

oil	36%	⎫
coal	28%	⎬ fosl fuel
nat gas	17%	⎭
wood, garbg/refuse	19%	
H$_2$O (hydropower)	1%	

Unit 5
Population Movements

3. *Do You Know These Words?*

1. social changes (d)

2. shifts (g)

3. sunbelt (h)

4. rural areas (a)

5. surpassed (c)

6. urban areas (b)

7. in terms of (i)

8. dramatic (e)

9. overall (f)

5. *Identify the Focus*

1. From 1970 to 1980, rural areas in the United States surpassed urban areas in terms of the rate of population growth. (These are the words on the tape.)

2. From 1970 to 1980, urban areas in the United States surpassed rural areas in terms of the rate of population growth. (This sentence is not the same as the other three because of the position of the words *urban* and *rural*.)

3. In the decade of the 70s, the rate of population growth in the nonmetropolitan regions of the country exceeded the rate of growth in the metropolitan areas. (This sentence is similar in meaning to sentences one and four.)

4. The rate of population growth in rural America was greater than that in urban America from 1970 to 1980. (This sentence is similar in meaning to sentences one and three.)

6. *Making Notes: The Focus*

1970–80 rural pop ↑ > urb pop

Abbreviated

population, urban

Words Left Out

from, to, areas, in, the, United States, surpassed, areas, in terms of, the rate of, growth

Symbols

↑ , >

7. Making Notes: The Supporting Details

1. NE — city 1.8% ↓ rural + 12.8%

2. NC — city 2.2% ↓ rural + 8%

3. W — city 21.9% ↑ rural + 32.2%

4. S — city 21.2% ↑ rural + 17.8%

Unit 6
A Child's Motor Skills

3. Do You Know These Words?

1. pattern (g)

2. prenatal (b)

3. stage (d)

4. motor skills development (e)

5. motor skills (a)

6. sequence (h)

7. exact (c)

8. specific (f)

5. Identify the Focus

1. A child's motor skills are usually developed in a certain sequence. (These are the words on the tape.)

2. Children's motor skills are usually learned in a predictable order. (This sentence has a similar meaning to sentence one.)

3. The sequence in which a baby learns physical movements generally follows a certain order. (This sentence has a similar meaning to sentence one.)

4. Children learn motor skills in many different sequences. (This sentence is the opposite of the other three sentences.)

6. Making Notes: The Focus

chld's motor skills—devel'd certn seq

Abbreviated
child's
developed
certain
sequence

Words Left Out
a, are, usually, in, a

Symbols
—

7. Making Notes: The Supporting Details

Skills	Age
holds chin up	1 mo
reaches fr obj	3 mos
holds on to thgs	6 mos
sits alone	7 mos
wlks w help	11 mos
climbs	13 mos
wlks alone	15 mos

Unit 7
Completing High School

3. Do You Know These Words?

1. assume (e)

2. natural (g)

3. majority (d)

4. complete (c)

5. that has not always been the case (f)

6. rose (h)

7. slightly (a)

8. figures (b)

5. Identify the Focus

1. From 1950 on, there has been a rise in the percentage of men and women who finish high school in the U.S. (This sentence has a similar meaning to sentences three and four.)

2. Since 1950, the total percentage of graduates from American high schools has remained constant. (This sentence does not have a similar meaning to the other three and does not give the meaning of the rising percentage on the graph.)

3. The percentage of adults who have completed high school in this country has increased since 1950. (These are the words on the tape.)

4. The percentage of adults without high school diplomas has decreased from 1950 to 1981. (This sentence is similar in meaning to sentences one and three, but does not give the meaning of the graph.)

6. Making Notes: The Focus

% adlts who hav compltd h.s ↑ 1950–81

Abbreviated

adults
have
completed
high school

Words Left Out

the, of, in, this, country, has, increased, since

Symbols

%, ↑

7. Making Notes: The Supporting Details

Year	Percentage
1950	38%
1960	42%
1970	60%
1975	69%
1981	77%

Unit 8
Large Families

3. Do You Know These Words?

1. fluctuation (c)

2. attitude (f)

3. favored (b)

4. decline (d)

5. sharp (h)

6. slight (a)

7. factors (e)

8. affect (g)

5. Identify the Focus

1. Feelings about having a large family have remained about the same in the U.S. (This sentence is opposite in meaning from the other three. The line on the graph would not go up and down if "remained the same" were true.)

2. Over the years people in this country have felt differently about having large families. (This sentence is similar in meaning to sentences three and four.)

3. People's attitudes in favor of big families have gone up and down. (This sentence is similar in meaning to sentences two and four.)

4. There's been a general fluctuation of attitude towards large families in the U.S. (These are the words on the tape.)

6. Making Notes: The Focus

US attit ↑ ↓ re: large fam

Abbreviated
the United States
attitude
families
re: (regarding = towards)

Words Left Out
There, has, been, a, general, fluctuation, of, in, the

Symbols

↑, ↓

7. Making Notes: The Supporting Details

Year	Percentage
1936	34%
1945	49%
1957	38%
1960	45%
1966	35%
1968	41%
1977	13%
1978	17%

Unit 9
A Cracker House

3. Do You Know These Words?

1. a native (c)
2. form (g)
3. function (h)
4. an attic (d)
5. elements (e)
6. the environment (f)
7. an adaptation (a)
8. a manifestation (b)

5. Identify the Focus

1. Crackers have developed a kind of architecture that exemplifies the concept that form follows function. (These are the words that are on the tape.)

2. First crackers built formal houses, then functional houses. (This sentence is different in meaning from the other three. The speaker is talking about only one style of house.)

3. The design of a cracker house matches the use of the house. (This sentence is similar in meaning to sentences one and four.)

4. When you look at a cracker house, you can see that form and function are very closely related. (This sentence is similar in meaning to sentences one and three.)

6. Making Notes: The Focus

Crackrs hav develpd architctr: form follows fnctn.

Abbreviated

crackers
have
developed
architecture
function

Words Left Out

a, kind, of, that, exemplifies, the, concept, that

Symbols

:

7. Making Notes: The Supporting Details

Form	Function
very high roof	hous cool as possbl
extnd porch arnd hous	sleepg in hot weathr
hgt abov grnd level	air circul & protect agnst varmints
roof overhang house	protect agnst rain
	satisfacty housg undr wthr conditn of southland

Unit 10
Immigration to Hawaii

3. Do You Know These Words?

1. unique (h)

2. in that (a)

3. at the state level (b)

4. rather than (f)

5. nonnative speaking immigrants (g)

6. broad (c)

7. category (d)

8. catch-all category (e)

9. What are the implications of these statistics? (i)

5. Identify the Focus

1. All other states have special problems in education similar to Hawaii's. (This sentence is not similar in meaning because the problems in Hawaii are *different from* other states.)

2. Hawaii has a number of special problems in the area of education. (These are the words on the tape.)

3. Hawaiian education has some problems that educational systems in other states don't share. (This sentence is similar in meaning to sentences two and four.)

4. Some of the problems in Hawaiian public education are different from problems in other state school systems. (This sentence is similar in meaning to sentences two and three.)

6. Making Notes: The Focus

HI has # spec probs in educa'n

Abbreviated
Hawaii
special
problems
education

Words Left Out
a, the, area, of

Symbols
#

7. Making Notes: The Supporting Details

HI has # spec probs in educ

1. sys at state lev not city/cnty

2. largest % of non-nat spkg immig/pop.

3. larg % attnd priv not pub school

e.g. look @ 70s

1. 6 grps
   a. Phil   38,389
   b. Kor   11,239
   c. Chin & Tai   4,618
   d. Japn   4,700
   e. Can   921
   f. Othrs   11,852

2. Wht ar implica'n of stats fr chld in clssrm?

Unit 11
The Demographic Transition

3. *Do You Know These Words?*

1. demographers (d)

2. the birth rate (f)

3. the death rate (g)

4. the demographic pattern (h)

5. a nation is developing (b)

6. the health care practices (i)

7. survive (c)

8. dramatically (e)

9. transition (a)

5. *Identify the Focus*

1. All countries change their birth rates and death rates in the same way. (This sentence does not have a similar meaning to the other three. The pattern is a general pattern. It does not mean every country is the same.)

2. Most countries have similar changes of birth rates and death rates as they develop. (This sentence is similar in meaning to sentences three and four.)

3. The demographic pattern is pretty predictable in developing nations. (These are the words on the tape.)

4. When countries become more modern, there is a usual pattern
   of change in how many babies are born and how many people die.
   (This sentence is similar in meaning to sentences two and three.)

6. Making Notes: The Focus

demogra'c pattrn predic'bl in devel'g nat'ns

Abbreviated

demographic
pattern
predictable
developing
nations

Words Left Out

The, is, pretty,

Symbols

'

7. Making Notes: The Supporting Details

def. demogphrs = peop who stdy # of peop who live/die

per populat'n

1st stage	hi birth rate/hi death rate
Why?	poor medic'n, poor health prac . . . peop don't live
2nd stage	hi birth rate, low death rate
Why?	betr health pract, new med'n, more food
3rd stage	lowr birth rate, low'r death rate
Why?	betr educa'n, betr health pract,

Unit 12
The Advantages of Exporting

3. Do You Know These Words?

1. summarize (h)

2. advantages (c)

3. new market opportunities (f)

4. customers (g)

5. the life, the recognition, and the acceptance of the company's products (d)

6. corporate growth (a)

7. production schedules (b)

8. production resources (e)

9. personnel (i)

5. Identify the Focus

1. And now I'd like to summarize some of the advantages for small businesses getting into the export business. (These are the words on the tape.)

2. At this point, I'd like to pull together the main reasons exporting is a good idea for small companies. (This sentence is similar in meaning to sentences one and four.)

3. Next I'd like to go into a little more detail about the advantages of international trade for small businesses. (This sentence is different from the other three. The speaker is going to explain, not summarize, the advantages.)

4. So the main reasons it's useful for a company to think about exporting can be summed up this way. (This sentence is similar in meaning to sentences one and two.)

6. Making Notes: The Focus

summz advan fr sm bus of exprt bus

Abbreviated
summarize
advantages
exporting
for
small
businesses

Words Left Out
and, now, I'd, like, to, some, the, getting, into, the

7. Making Notes: The Supporting Details

1. mkts   new mkt opporty i.e. forgn cntries

2. custmrs   mor custmrs —— co's prods

3. prod life   life, recogni'n & accept of prods —— longr time

4. corp. growth   co can exper corp growth/expnd invest/financ opportnties

5. planning   plan mor efficntly, use prodctn facil & peop mor effectivly

Unit 13
Government Expenditures

3. Do You Know These Words?

1. government expenditures (e)

2. the current budget (h)

3. direct payments to individuals (d)

4. national defense (b)

5. direct grants (c)

6. interest payments (f)

7. the leftover category (i)

8. the current administration (j)

9. balance the budget (a)

10. make any cuts (g)

5. Identify the Focus

1. Right now the government budgets tax dollars for five kinds of expenses. (This sentence is similar in meaning to sentences two and three.)

2. There are five categories of government expenditures in the current budget. (These are the words that are on the tape.)

3. There are five categories of government revenues in the current budget. (This sentence is different in meaning from the other three since revenues means money the government collects, i.e., taxes.)

4. The national budget reveals five main categories of expenditures. (This sentence is similar in meaning to sentences one and three.)

6. *Making Notes: The Focus*

5 categ of expenditr in curr budgt

Abbreviated

categories
expenditures
current
budget

Words Left Out

there, are, government, the

Symbols

5

7. *Making Notes: The Supporting Details*

dir pmts to indiv	42%
nat'l defen	27%
dir grants cities/stat	12%
int pmts	11%
other	8%

What is the speaker's reason for telling these statistics to the professor (and her class)? Use your own note forms to write down the speaker's two questions.

1. can u explain how the curr admin is plan'g to bal budget whn they're not going to make cuts?

2. how are we going to handl the sit?

Perhaps the speaker is trying to use current statistics to make her question stronger.

Unit 14
Ecosystems

3. *Do You Know These Words?*

1. an interrelated system (a)

2. made up of (h)

3. a community (e)

4. a cycle of life (i)

5. pool of nutrients (f)

6. enable (b)

7. herbivores (c)

8. exotic (j)

9. counterparted with (g)

10. carnivores (d)

11. decay organisms (k)

5. Identify the Focus

1. A community of animals, plants, and bacteria forms an unrelated system called an ecosystem. (This sentence is different from the other three because the word "unrelated" is opposite in meaning from interrelated.)

2. A group of animals, plants, and bacteria forming an interconnected system is called an ecosystem. (This sentence is similar in meaning to sentences three and four.)

3. An ecosystem is an interrelated system made up of a community of animals, plants, and bacteria. (These are the words on the tape.)

4. Ecosystem describes the interrelationships of a community of animals, plants, and bacteria. (This sentence is similar in meaning to sentences two and three.)

6. Making Notes: The Focus

ecosys = interrelatd sys = commty of anim/plants/bact

Abbreviated
ecosystem
interrelatd
system
community
animals
bacteria

Words Left Out
An, is, an, made up of, a, and

Symbols

=

7. Making Notes: The Supporting Details

1. strtg pt the pool of nutrnts = minerals fr plants

2. plant-eatg anim = herbivore

3. exotc anim = carn = pandas, koalas

4. meat-eatg anim (carnivores) eat herb.

5. sm meat-eatr eat othr meat eatr

6. anim + plants — die — decay organisms — nutrients

sun's energy prod heat — makes plants grw

Unit 15
International Student Survey

3. Do You Know These Words?

1. a survey form (d)

2. categories (f)

3. listed in rank order (k)

4. adjustment problems (i)

5. meeting financial expenses (e)

6. budgeting time (h)

7. get involved in campus activities (g)

8. studying efficiently (j)

9. a critical thinker (c)

10. an independent thinker (b)

11. the ERIC system (a)

5. Identify the Focus

1. Foreign students evaluate possible problems with study in the U.S. (This sentence is similar in meaning to sentences two and four.)

2. International students rank the adjustment problems to American study. (These are the words on the tape.)

3. Problems for international students concern many American colleges. (This sentence is different from the other three sentences. The students were surveyed, not the colleges.)

4. The survey reveals the ranking of adjustments to study in America by a group of international students. (This sentence is similar in meaning to sentences one and two.)

6. *Making Notes: The Focus*

internatl studs rank adjust probs to Am study

Abbreviated
international
students
adjustment
problems
American

Words Left Out
the

7. *Making Notes: The Supporting Details*

1. Meeting financial expenses	24%
2. Budgeting time	14%
3. Earning satisfactory grades	13%
4. Deciding whether or how much to get involved in campus activities	13%
5. Studying efficiently	10%
6. Becoming a more critical and independent thinker	9%
7. Selecting a field of study and/or a career	8%
8. Meeting and knowing other students	6%

Unit 16
Jobs for Women and Men

3. *Do You Know These Words?*

1. make that statement (k)

2. decade (i)

3. table (j)

4. in managerial positions (c)

5. whereas (b)

6. occupied (d)

7. distressing (m)

8. statistic (g)

9. production supervisors (h)

10. assemblers (n)

11. down at the bottom of the heap (e)

12. the only conclusion we can draw (a)

13. occupational positions of authority (f)

14. dominated (l)

5. Identify the Focus

1. The jobs having authority continue to be mostly held by men. (This sentence is similar in meaning to sentences two and three.)

2. Males still work in the jobs with the most authority. (This sentence is similar in meaning to sentences one and three.)

3. The occupational positions of authority continue to be dominated by males. (These are the words on the tape.)

4. The occupational positions of authority will continue to be dominated by males. (This sentence is different in meaning from the other three sentences. The word "will" implies that the situation will continue in the future.)

6. Making Notes: The Focus

occupa'nl pos of auth — dom by ♂ in this socty

Abbreviated

occupational
positions
authority
dominated

Words Left Out

The, continue, to, be

Symbols

—, ♂

7. Making Notes: The Supporting Details

Occupation	Number of Men	Percentage of Women
Managers	3,824,609	26.9%
Production Supervisors	1,605,489	15.0%
Assemblers	858,542	49.5%
Cooks	578,320	57.2%
Elementary	569,823	75.4%

Unit 17
USA Today

3. Do You Know These Words?

1. edited (h)
2. composed (i)
3. satellite (a)
4. sites (f)
5. facsimile machines (b)
6. laser scanners (c)
7. the equator (l)
8. high resolution (o)
9. laser beam (g)
10. scans (j)
11. beamed (k)
12. antenna (e)
13. exposes the film (n)
14. processed (m)
15. plate (d)

5. Identify the Focus

1. It's modern technology that allows *USA Today* to publish a national newspaper. (This sentence is similar in meaning to sentences two and three.)

2. *USA Today* can publish a nationwide daily paper because of modern technology. (This sentence is similar in meaning to sentences one and three.)

3. Without this modern technology, it would be impossible for *USA Today* to publish a national daily newspaper. (These are the words on the tape.)

4. With *USA Today's* modern technology, it's impossible to publish a national daily newspaper. (This sentence is different in meaning from the other three sentences. *USA Today's* modern technology makes a national daily paper possible, not impossible.)

6. Making Notes: The Focus

w/o mod tech — imposs to pub nat daily news

Abbreviated

without
modern
technology
impossible
publish
national
newspaper

Words Left Out

this, it, would, be, for, *USA Today*, a,

Symbols

/, —

7. Making Notes: The Supporting Details

1. chg pages incl photos — electnc impulses

2. impulses — satellite @ spd of light

3. sat beams to prntg ctrs

4. antennas catch impulses

5. chg impuls to light thru fax mach & laser scanners

6. light exposes negs = newspaper pg size

7. negs make plates — newspaper

Unit 18
Adjusting to College Life

3. *Do You Know These Words?*

1. on this campus (c)
2. reassure you (l)
3. adjustment problems (j)
4. academic problems (k)
5. signed up for (f)
6. registration (m)
7. everything was filled (b)
8. term papers (g)
9. personal problems (h)
10. miserable (p)
11. dorm (e)
12. social problems (i)
13. eventually (a)
14. work out (d)
15. struggling (o)
16. overwhelming (n)

5. *Identify the Focus*

1. All international students have some adjustment problems while studying here. (These are the words on the tape.)

2. All students from abroad report some problems adjusting while a student here. (This sentence is similar in meaning to sentences one and four.)

3. All students have some problems getting used to things as a student here. (This sentence is different in meaning from the other three. It mentions all students, not just international students.)

4. Problems of adjustment are part of student life for all foreign students who study here. (This sentence is similar in meaning to sentences one and two.)

6. Making Notes: The Focus

all internt'l studs → sm adjust probs here

Abbreviated
international
students
some
adjustment
problems

Words Left Out
have, while studying

Symbols
→

7. Making Notes: The Supporting Details

1. academic problems
   e.g., sign up for wrong course, classes filled, take classes I don't want, problems with English, knowing how to study, writing term papers

2. personal problems
   e.g., loneliness, noisy dorms, expensive apartments, landlords won't rent to students/don't like foreign students

3. social problems
   e.g., don't have friends from home nearby, problems making new friends, having dating problems

1. acad probs
   e.g., sign up fr wrong course, classes filled, take classes don't want, probs w Eng, knowg how to stud, writg term papers

2. persl probs
   e.g., loneliness, noisy dorms, $$ apts, landlords won't rent to stud/ don't like FS

3. socl probs
   e.g., don't have friends from home, probs making new friends, dating probs

Unit 19
Recycling Waste Water

3. Do You Know These Words?

1. environment (b)
2. recycle (k)
3. waste materials (c)
4. otherwise (h)
5. pollute (j)
6. schemes (o)
7. industrial processes (p)
8. methane gas (l)
9. bacteria (q)
10. an anaerobic process (a)
11. nutrients (e)
12. feed on (g)
13. filter (m)
14. blanket (f)
15. outlet (d)
16. sewage treatment plant (n)
17. receives further purification (i)

5. Identify the Focus

1. A bacteria process recovers beer and waste water from a treatment tank. (This sentence is different in meaning from the other three sentences. Gas and clear water are recovered from waste water.)

2. Recycling waste water through a bacteria process produces clear water and useful methane gas for the company. (This sentence is similar in meaning to sentences three and four.)

3. The beer company that we're looking at changes waste water into methane gas and clear water. (These are the words that are on the tape.)

4. Waste water recycled from beer production yields methane gas and clear water. (This sentence is similar in meaning to sentences two and three.)

6. Making Notes: The Focus

beer co chgs waste $H_2O \rightarrow$ CH4 + clr H_2O

Abbreviated
company
changes
clear

Words Left Out
the, that, we're, looking, at, into

Symbols
H_2O, $\rightarrow$, CH4, +

7. Making Notes: The Supporting Details

beer co chgs waste $H_2O \rightarrow$ CH4 + clr H_2O

1. waste $H_2O \rightarrow$ bottm tank

2. bact feeds on nutrnts/mats in waste H_2O

3. 4/5 hrs fr H_2O ↑ thru bact

4. 2 prods: clr H_2O + CH4

5. CH4 $\rightarrow$ beer co $\rightarrow$ use fr htg

6. clr $H_2O \rightarrow$ sewage treatmnt plant $\rightarrow$ re-use again

Unit 20
The Scientific Method

3. Do You Know These Words?

1. our formal course (n)

2. getting a grip on (e)

3. distinct (l)

4. define a problem (d)

5. throw one out (i)

6. figure out (o)

7. review the literature (k)

8. formulate a hypothesis (c)

9. analyze (f)

10. data (g)

11. conduct a survey (a)

12. conclusion (h)

13. puts us on to (j)

14. research (m)

15. study (p)

16. investigation (b)

5. *Identify the Focus*

1. Five separate steps are followed when using the scientific method. (This sentence is similar in meaning to sentences three and four.)

2. Scientists use five distinct methods in their experiments. (This sentence is different in meaning from the other three. There is one method with five parts, not five methods.)

3. There are five distinct steps within the scientific method. (These are the words that are on the tape.)

4. The scientific method consists of five different steps. (This sentence is similar in meaning to sentences one and three.)

6. *Making Notes: The Focus*

scientc meth → 5 steps

Abbreviated
scientific
method

Words Left Out
there, are, five, distinct, within, the

Symbols
5, →

7. *Making Notes: The Supporting Details*

scientfc meth → 5 steps

1. def prob

2. rev lit

3. form hypoths

4. coll & analz data
   a. expermnt
   b. survy

5. devlp conclu'n

Unit 21
Persuasion in Speaking

3. Do You Know These Words?

1. invent (f)

2. compile (j)

3. encounter (l)

4. gruesome (e) ·

5. colleague (a)

6. ethnicity (k)

7. superficial (g)

8. component (i)

9. slick (c)

10. impediment (b)

11. analysis (d)

12. frosting (m)

13. crucial (n)

14. valid (h)

5. Identify the Focus

1. Aristotle enumerated three kinds of persuasion. (This sentence is similar in meaning to sentences two and three.)

2. Aristotle says there are basically three types of persuasion. (These are the words on the tape.)

3. There are three different ways to convince someone of something,

according to Aristotle. (This sentence is similar in meaning to sentences one and two.)

4. There are three types of speeches, according to Aristotle. (This sentence is different in meaning from the other three.)

6. Making Notes: The Focus

Arist → 3 kinds per

Abbreviated
Aristotle, persuasion

Words Left Out
says, there, are, basically, types, of

Symbols
→, 3

7. Making Notes: The Supporting Details

1. Ethos — defined as: ethical appeal/credibility
   e.g. person's sex, age, dress, ethnic origin, organization, delivery

2. Pathos — defined as: pathetic/appeal to emotions
   e.g. showing pictures of abused children

3. Logos — defined as: logical/appeal to reason
   e.g. give statistics

Unit 22
The Basic Accounting Formula

3. Do You Know These Words?

1. keeping track of (k)

2. hint (d)

3. tool (e)

4. seesaw (a)

5. accountants (j)

6. assets (m)

7. inventory (o)

8. fixtures (l)

9. tend to (f)

10. debt (g)

11. liabilities (c)

12. investment (b)

13. analogy (h)

14. equity (n)

15. derivative of (i)

5. Identify the Focus

1. The accounting formula which is fundamental is that one's assets are equal to one's liabilities and equity. (This sentence is similar in meaning to sentences three and four.)

2. The basic accounting formula can be stated in the following: liabilities equal assets plus equity. (This sentence is different in meaning from the other three sentences. Liabilities equal assets minus equity.)

3. The fundamental accounting formula is that all that we own is equal to a combination of our debts and investments. (This sentence is similar in meaning to sentences one and four.)

4. Your basic accounting equation: assets equal liabilities plus equity. (These are the words on the tape.)

6. Making Notes: The Focus

$A = L + E$

Abbreviated
assets/liabilities/equity

Words Left Out
your, basic accounting, equation

Symbols
=, +

7. Making Notes: The Supporting Details

Assets: inventory, fixtures, equipment, money

Liabilities: debt coming from credit purchases

Equity: owner's/partner's/stockholder's

Unit 23
Nutrition

3. Do You Know These Words?

1. nutrients (f)

2. poultry (g)

3. zip (a)

4. function (l)

5. complex (h)

6. concentrated (o)

7. calories (k)

8. excess (n)

9. deficiency (j)

10. cheat (d)

11. can't stand (i)

12. hit (m)

13. osteoporosis (b)

14. osteomalacia (c)

15. caries (e)

5. Identify the Focus

1. There are six various kinds of nutrients that are spoken about in the course of a year. (This sentence is similar in meaning to sentences two and four.)

2. The six different food groups are discussed during the year. (This sentence is similar in meaning to sentences one and four.)

3. What we talk about all during the year are six different ways to eat. (This sentence is different in meaning from the other three sentences. Six different ways to eat is not the same as six classes of nutrients.)

4. What we talk about all during the year are the six classes of nutrients. (These are the words on the tape.)

6. Making Notes: The Focus

Nut → 6 class

Abbreviated

nutrients
classes

Words Left Out

What, we, talk, about, all, during, the, year, are, the, of

Symbols

→

7. Making Notes: The Supporting Details

1. Protein
   e.g. meat/fish/poultry/milk/eggs/cheese/beans/nuts
   Reason imp: build/repair/maintain body

2. Carbohydrates
   e.g. rice/bread/cereals/potatoes
   Reason imp: supply energy

3. Fats
   e.g. butter/margarine/cream/mayonnaise/peanut butter
   Reason imp: supply energy

4. Minerals
   e.g. calcium — foods made from milk
                  small fish with bones
                  dark green leafy vegetables
       iron — liver, spinach
   Reason imp: strong bones and teeth/good for blood

5. Vitamins

6. Water

Unit 24
The Law of Demand

3. Do You Know These Words?

1. determines (c)

2. exists (h)

3. flea market (i)

4. motivated (e)

5. forces (g)

6. afford (f)

7. factor (d)

8. purchasing patterns (a)

9. isolate (j)

10. key (l)

11. variable (k)

12. determinant (b)

5. Identify the Focus

1. What are the forces that motivate you to use credit cards for something? (This sentence is different in meaning from the other three sentences. Credit cards were not mentioned.)

2. What are the influences which cause you to buy something? (This sentence is similar in meaning to sentences three and four.)

3. What motivates you to buy something? (These are the words on the tape.)

4. What reasons do you have for purchasing something? (This sentence is similar in meaning to sentences two and three.)

6. Making Notes: The Focus

What motiv buy X

Abbreviated

motivates

Words Left Out

you, to, something

Symbols

X

7. Making Notes: The Supporting Details

taste/preference
how much income you have
prices of related goods
*price of good itself

Unit 25
The Judicial System

3. Do You Know These Words?

1. arson (i)	6. plead (c)
2. embezzlement (j)	7. verdict (f)
3. violate (a)	8. defendant (g)
4. preliminary (b)	9. penitentiary (h)
5. sufficient (d)	10. impose sentence (e)

5. Identify the Focus

1. What are the procedures for dealing with an individual who has committed a serious crime? (This sentence is similar in meaning to sentences two and four.)

2. What happens to a person when they are arrested for a felony offense? (These are the words on the tape.)

3. What occurs when somebody is arrested for committing a misdemeanor? (This sentence is different in meaning from the other three sentences. A misdemeanor is not a serious crime.)

4. When someone has broken an important law, how does the judicial system handle that person? (This sentence is similar in meaning to sentences one and two.)

6. Making Notes: The Focus

What hap per when arrest fel off

Abbreviated
happens, person, arrested, felony, offense

Words Left Out
to, a, they, are, for, a

7. Making Notes: The Supporting Details

Person Arrested → Inferior Court → Preliminary Hearing →

Trial → Sentencing → Penitentiary